D1636341

What's Your Sign?

What's Your Sign?

A Guide to Astrology
for the Cosmically Curious

SANCTUARY™

Andrews McMeel
PUBLISHING®

What's Your Sign? copyright © 2022 by Sanctuary Ventures, Inc. All rights reserved.
Printed in China. No part of this book may be used or reproduced in any manner whatsoever
without written permission except in the case of reprints in the context of reviews.

Andrews McMeel Publishing
a division of Andrews McMeel Universal
1130 Walnut Street, Kansas City, Missouri 64106

www.andrewsmcmeel.com

22 23 24 25 26 SDB 10 9 8 7 6 5 4 3 2 1

ISBN: 978-1-5248-7155-0

Library of Congress Control Number: 2021945160

Editor: Hannah Dussold
Art Director/Designer: Holly Swayne
Production Editor: Dave Shaw
Production Manager: Tamara Haus

ATTENTION: SCHOOLS AND BUSINESSES
Andrews McMeel books are available at quantity discounts with bulk purchase
for educational, business, or sales promotional use. For information, please e-mail
the Andrews McMeel Publishing Special Sales Department:
specialsales@amuniversal.com.

Contents

Welcome to the Stars

So you want to know more about astrology? You're in the right place. Everyone loves a good astrology meme, but astrology goes so much deeper than stereotypes and simplifications. The details that make horoscopes and memes resonate deeply are tied to the particulars of how the many parts of your personal astrology interact. Did you know you have more than one astrological sign or that each planet plays a role in understanding your personality?

Astrology can seem complicated to explore, but with a good map, you can navigate the basics with ease. Your birth chart is your unique and personal map of the stars. It reveals so much more than what your sun sign (what we typically see in horoscopes) does. What do you need to know to unlock the nuances of your birth chart?

That's what we're here to share!

Astrology can offer guidance and insight into so many more parts of your life than you may realize. If you're just reading your daily horoscope, you may relate (or not!) to only your sun sign, which you know from your birthday. You might wonder why some aspects of your horoscope don't exactly fit your personality. Spoiler: your personality is influenced by so many other astrological players. In fact, you've got a sign for every planet in our solar system. Maybe you're an introverted Leo, and you're always mystified by astrologers talking about how much you love the spotlight. But maybe you have a Pisces moon and you're a Cancer rising, and suddenly it makes perfect sense that you're slower to warm up to the world around you.

Now, if all of that seemed like a mystical word salad that you have no idea about, have no fear. All of our astrological secrets will be revealed in due time!

Speaking of time, we intend for you to have a good one while you're reading this book. We've broken the book down into sections that will guide you through the basics and give you the tools you need to decode the stars. We'll dig into the twelve signs of the zodiac, complete with infographics and illustrations to help you bring the stars down to earth and into your life on a practical, everyday level. We'll also dig into some astrology basics (what are houses, anyway?) to give you the inside scoop that guides astrologers both on- and off-line. Our goal is to make sure we're all on the same page about why this ancient practice still has relevance for our lives today.

THE HISTORY OF ASTROLOGY

Astrology has been around for thousands of years, and practically every ancient culture independently developed its own zodiac system. This is no small historical coincidence. The fact that so many ancient cultures developed whole systems to tease out how these distant celestial bodies influenced our lives here on little ol' planet Earth points to something deep about what it means to be a person in this universe. Imagine the world with no streetlights or headlights, no lamps or screens. The stars were the only thing to draw curious nocturnal eyes upward. Only those little pinpricks of slow-moving starlight twinkling away, night after night, in awe-inspiring patterns. If you've ever lain outside on the grass on a warm summer night trying to find the Big Dipper, you've experienced a small taste of the wonder that sparked this worldwide fascination with astrology.

Let's start at the beginning, like way back in the day (we're talking the BC days). Originally, scholars studied astrology and astronomy side by side: astronomy was studying the stars, and astrology was interpreting what those positions meant. Early astronomy texts provided scientific contributions, like accurately timing the transits of the planets in the sky (which still stun modern-day scientists with their crazy-high levels of astronomical accuracy). They also included astrological interpretations of what these movements meant for human life. Eventually, the two disciplines parted ways, but the language they use occasionally overlaps even today. This is why you might see a panic over "new zodiac signs" or astrophysicists weighing in on astrology. The two studies are sisters, not twins, and much like your eyebrows, they frame how we see the stars in our eyes.

The system that we use today is designated as tropical (or "Western") astrology and traces its roots back to Persia around 475 BC. The other ancient systems you might still hear about today are the Chinese zodiac, which is based on the year you were born (e.g., "Year of the Dragon"), and Vedic ("Eastern" or sidereal) astrology, which originated in modern-day India and bases the zodiac on a relationship to space rather than time. Does this sound too far out? Don't worry, we're going to stick to what we know best here, which is the tropical astrology you already know and love (even if you didn't know the name). But it's important to know there's more than one way of interpreting the stars!

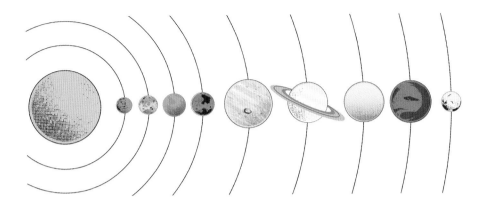

Just as the systems for interpreting the cosmos differ from place to place, they also differ across the ages. Astrology has evolved and expanded over the centuries (like all practices that deal with the unseen logics of life and have roots in antiquity). Generally, the focus of astrology used to be the *conditions* of someone's life. Now, with the strong influence of psychoanalysis and our culture of self-help, therapy, and personal development, the study of the stars focuses on the *psychological interior* of your life. "What does my birth chart reveal about me?" is not a question Queen Elizabeth I would have asked her personal astrologer, John Dee. She was more likely to ask how the planets would influence the political machinations of her reign.

Today, we scroll through Instagram to read astrology memes that might help us discover more about ourselves and pore over our birth charts with like-minded friends. This is the other change that astrology has seen in the last few decades: it has experienced the expansive influence of the internet boom. Led by Susan Miller and her in-depth horoscopes at Astrology Zone in the mid-90s, astrologers went online, and a practice relegated to a small newspaper column or phone hotline suddenly had a much wider audience. Where astrologers used to painstakingly calculate charts and draw them for clients by hand, you can now get your birth chart for free online simply by plugging in your information. (Check out the back of this book for information on how to download the Sanctuary app!) Suddenly, anyone has access to their chart. With the dawn of social media, astrology has gone viral, revolutionizing the astrology industry—making the practice more democratic, more social, but also more prone to miscommunication and misinformation.

Social media has seen explosive growth, and with it has come the rise of the astrology app and the astrology meme. Personalized horoscopes can be delivered straight to your phone before you're even out of bed, no newspaper required. Comprehensive birth chart interpretations are done in real-time by expert astrologers who are only a click away, all from the comfort of your couch. One thing stays the same: the more you can understand for yourself, the more empowered you will be to embrace your cosmic curiosity and explore the cosmos for yourself, through yourself.

NAVIGATING A BIRTH CHART

What is a birth chart? Great question! You win! Okay, fine, learning the basics of astrology is a little more involved than that. But asking that question is the first step, and the journey is fun and magical, so yes, you have already won in a sense. So, winner, the answer to your question is that a birth chart is a kind of personal map that captures exactly what the sky looked like the moment you were born.

Your chart is unique to you. It is highly specific and describes the shape of cosmic relations not only where you were born, but when you were born—down to the precise minute you entered this world! Think of it this way: there are lots of people with your sun sign, but how many of them were born in that city, at that exact moment, with the precise combination of everything in your chart that conspires to give you your unique self?

Now we're getting into why you might not *perfectly* relate to every other person who shares your sun sign. A birth chart captures your uniqueness. That is why we say that your sun sign is just the start! You only need to know your birthday in order to know your sun sign. To go deeper, you'll need to know where you were born and the time you were born. As far as the time goes, you can round to the nearest half-hour if you need to. Not all of us know this info off the top of our heads, so take a second to text your parents or check your birth certificate to find out. We'll wait (but tell your mom or dad we said hi!).

Okay, now that you have all the details on your grand entrance into this world, you can put that info into a website or app (we've heard of this great one called

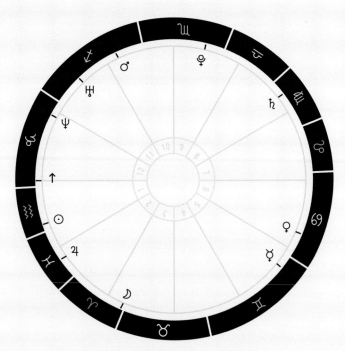

A basic birth chart with planets, signs, and houses.

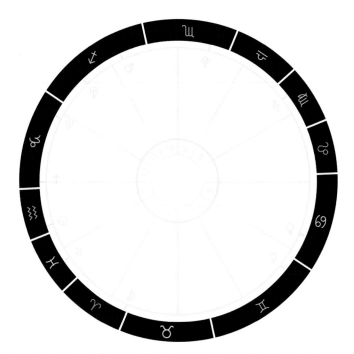

A birth chart has a ring of the astrological signs around the outside, in the order they appear throughout the calendar year.

Sanctuary Astrology that's available for iOS and Android) and the chart it generates is the celestial font of knowledge you'll be drinking from.

Let's talk about what you'll do with all the cosmic knowledge you're about to be the proud owner of—beginning with the planets. Each planet in our universe falls under the influence of a particular sign. The signs each go in order, starting with Aries and ending with Pisces, and they form a circle or wheel like a clock with each sign in its place. Think of that astrological wheel laid flat against the dome of the sky and stars, wrapped around the Earth. Each sign has a slice of sky that it "rules." This slice correlates roughly with the actual location of the constellation that names each of the twelve zodiac signs. When a planet falls in that section, they're said to be "in" that sign.

This is how you get your sun in Scorpio, your Venus in Capricorn, and every other placement in your birth chart. Oh, and about those placements—not only does every planet have a sign assigned to it based on where it was in the sky when you were born, but your chart also has a handful of other placements that we'll get into soon.

But before we dig into the placements, we need to mention houses briefly (though don't worry, we'll go deeper later, after you've had time to catch your breath). Any given birth chart is also organized by what astrologers call "houses": twelve different zones stretched evenly across the 360 degrees of a natal chart.

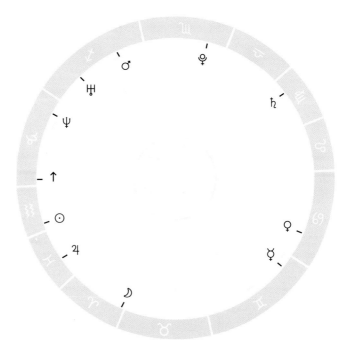

Inside the birth chart's segments you'll find symbols for each planet, plus a few bonus placements depending on where you find your chart.

Each of these houses corresponds to different areas of your life, like your relationships, home life, and career path. Think of them as houses in a neighborhood—all your planets live in the neighborhood, nearby one another. They each have personalities specific to you (that's the sign they occupy), but they "live" in that house and arrange the elements of your love life or your relationship to money as they see fit, according to their special home. You might already know a little about houses if you know your rising or ascendant sign, which was "rising" in the sky as you were born. That sign is always, always in your first house, and everything in your chart works out from that point.

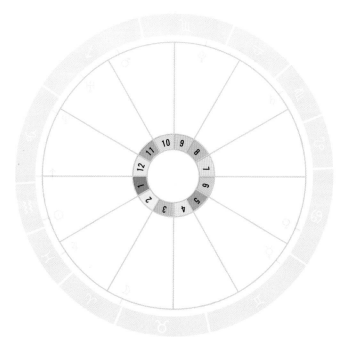

The sections within a birth chart's outlines are called houses, and they determine what part of your life each planet and sign has an impact.

With all that info crammed into one little chart, you may be asking yourself: What can't my chart tell me?! Well, a few things. Your birth chart can't tell you whether or not you will get that promotion. It can't tell you whether or not that cute barista likes you back. It also can't tell you the weather next week, the meaning of life, when to use a semicolon versus just a colon, etc. It's not that your birth chart is holding out on you—it's just that your birth chart can't take into account all of the myriad choices you get to make in life. Only you can decide what you'll do with all the astrological influences that are at play in your life. (Hello, free will!) Your birth chart is like a map of your spirit, psyche, and all the many destinies that are possible for you. Think of it like a factory setting that you control, shape, and use to craft your own adventure.

WHAT ASTROLOGERS DO

Phew. That's a LOT of information. Don't worry if you're confused or overwhelmed. You're not the only one! Most people, even die-hard astrology enthusiasts, don't know everything about how to read all the information and nuances of their birth chart. But when a professional astrologer reads your birth chart, they understand how to put these pieces together. They know that the sign a planet is in is not even half the picture, and what house a planet lives in is very important. They can bring us lots of other information we can't even begin to dive into here.

To truly understand the full complexity of your chart, there is even more information to consider, like how the planets interact together at specific angles (which astrologers call "aspects"). There is also the condition of the planet to consider; planets are at home in some signs, where they flow with natural ease, but they have to work a little harder in others. Don't sweat these details. Getting a reading with a professional astrologer puts all this information in context, curated for your concerns and questions, far beyond a simple (albeit fun!) sun-sign meme. We know it's a lot, so we're going to stick to the basics so you have a solid foundation. Then, if and when you chat with an astrologer, you can get the very most out of that conversation.

YOUR BIG THREE

Any exploration of a birth chart starts with the same foundation: an in-depth look at what we call your Big Three: your sun, moon, and rising signs. Your sun sign is the essence of your chart: your sense of self, your primary concerns. Your rising sign, or ascendant, is the essence of your external presence in the world and how others see you. Your moon sign represents your inner world and the emotional framework that you use to navigate life.

Beyond those three, most astrologers will be able to tell you about how each planet influences your life depending on how it's positioned relative to the other planets, about how the different areas in your life are shaped by the constellations present in any of the given houses, and about major themes in your life. But remember that whole history lesson about astrology being an umbrella term that encompasses ancient and diverse practices for understanding the relationship between humans and the stars? Yeah, that is an important tidbit to remember when we talk about professional astrologers and astrology at large.

In early astrological tradition, astrologers from Egypt, India, and China used astrology primarily in divination or communing with the divine, in service of the ruling class. Say a king or queen needed to know which rival they should become allies with, or whether or not the crops would thrive; they might turn to their friendly royal astrologer and seek guidance. Astrology then focused on the fixed stars in the sky, the ones that seemed to stay in the same place for a long time. They weren't too concerned with the day-to-day goings-on of the everyday common people like the rest of us (unless, of course, a king or queen is reading this right now, in which case, our apologies, Your Majesty).

This brings us to the last history lesson before we set you off on your journey through this book and toward astrological illumination. For our last lesson, we'll travel to Persia circa 475 BC when Persian astrologers changed up the game and developed—drumroll, please—a twelve-sign zodiac! And that, friends, was the beginning of the Big Three signs and all the dynamic personal planets taking on a starring (wink) role in the way we practice astrology.

There is no one correct tradition, and to claim the supremacy of one tradition over another does a disservice to the art's diverse history and contemporary expansion. It's important to recognize the roots of our particular tradition while also opening up the field to include other traditions on the same footing as the Western astrology we use. Scrolling through your Instagram liking a way-too-accurate astrology meme is only possible because of these complex histories.

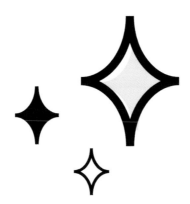

HOW TO USE THIS BOOK

If you've picked up this book, maybe you started your foray into astrology with casual memes or our infographics on social media, or maybe you've been in the astrology game for a while and simply want to dig deeper. No matter what brought you to these pages, we promise that reading through it will leave you richer in self-knowledge and empowered to find new meaning in astrology at large. We know that everybody starts at a different point with all of this, so we want to offer you a few different ways to use this book to prevent *total overwhelm* for astrology newbies, or to guide more experienced folks toward the parts of the astrological big picture that makes the most sense for them.

First, we're not like other astrology books. And sure, we know all the other astrology books say that, but let us tell you what we mean: We are going to be diving into all twelve signs, of course, as well as the basics to help you read your birth chart yourself. It's all about accessible, useful, and fun ways to apply the bigger ideas in astrology to your own life. We've included our signature infographics to give you imaginative starting points for how your particular sign's energy might manifest in your life circumstances. Like, sure—Gemini is super chatty and curious, but what does that look like in an everyday setting? When you walk into a party, what are the key ways to spot a Gemini sun in the wild? (Spoiler: they're probably the ones buzzing from group to group, stirring up intrigue and conversation.)

You'll come out of this book with a better understanding of your own chart and a couple of great jokes, to boot. However, it's important to remember that a quip about the sun in Gemini, for example, can't and doesn't take into account the various expressions that come with the specific placement of your Gemini sun: if it's in the first or fifth or seventh house; if it's right next to Mercury or Uranus; if it's right on your midheaven. Those specific nuances are *important*, and a one-on-one reading with an astrologer can help you dig into the layers of your birth chart.

Flip through the signs to bone up on the basics, or start on page one and read your way to the end. You can even pull up your chart and scan for specific placements you've got questions about, reviewing a planet and then combining its sign "personality" in your chart to get to know the rest of your chart better.

This book will give you everything you need to understand the basics and to start asking new questions (like, what the heck does "midheaven" mean, anyway, and do I have one? Should I get that checked out by a specialist?). For your convenience and delight, here are a few ways we recommend navigating your way through this book.

START WITH WHAT YOU KNOW

If you're reading this like, "Yeah, yeah, but tell me more about ME," go ahead and skip right to the sign profiles. Start with your sun sign and get your fill of details about your sign's basic traits and place in the zodiac, as well as your strengths, challenges, career stuff, and relationship styles. You'll also find info in these profiles about what each sign means when it's your sun sign as opposed to your moon or rising sign, which should set you merrily on your way toward the next level of astrological know-how.

LET YOUR CURIOSITY GUIDE YOU

For all the curious cats out there who want to learn more about specific elements of astrology (or for the slightly chaotic among us who just want to walk the road less traveled and discover stuff as you go along) you can flip through the book at will, or use the table of contents. Either one of these approaches is fine. We designed this book to be just as useful in small doses as it is if you read it cover to cover.

FOR THE OVERACHIEVERS . . .

Of course, there is always the option of reading this book the way we read most books . . . from beginning to end. Although this path might make some impatient, there are those of us who love to get the whole picture laid out for us in a nice, soothing, linear way. This is also a good way to use this book if you have aspirations of becoming an astrologer yourself one day. If you're one of these front-to-back readers, know that we also had you in mind while making this book, and we've set it up so that you'll learn everything you need to know in order. Think of this method as a ladder: like, we built you a ladder of astro-knowledge, and if you climb it steadily to the top you'll arrive at . . . the skies? Ultimate astrological wisdom? Fine, we don't know where the ladder metaphor ends, but by the time you finish this book, you'll definitely be able to impress all your friends.

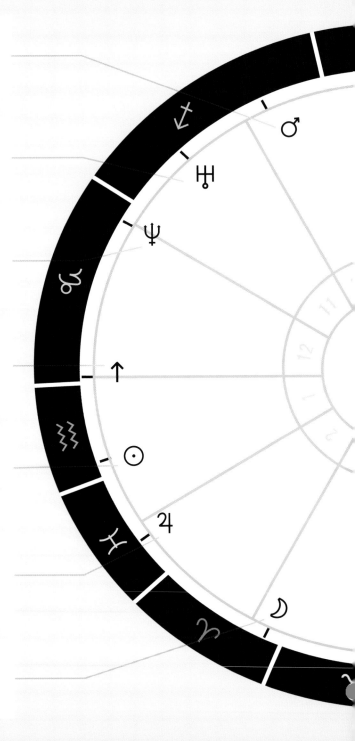

MARS

Your determination
and your passion

URANUS

Your innovation and
your rebellions

NEPTUNE

Your fantasies and
your imagination

RISING

Your perspective and
your decisions

SUN

Your sense of self and
your primary concerns

JUPITER

Your outlook and your
temptations

MOON

Your emotional world
and your self-care

PLUTO
Your power and your transformations

SATURN
Your discipline and your well-being

HOUSES
These important locations in your chart map the areas of your life that a planet or sign impacts

VENUS
Your values and your desires

MERCURY
Your mind and your speech

SIGNS
These familiar archetypes reveal how a planet's qualities are expressed in your chart

The Planets

THE LUMINARIES

SUN	MOON	RISING
"I AM"	"I FEEL"	"I SEE"
GOALS	BEHAVIORS	PERCEPTIONS
EXPRESSES	REFLECTS	UNDERSTANDS
WANTS	NEEDS	ACTS
IDENTITY	EMOTION	PRESENCE
☉	☽	↑

Before our days and nights were illuminated with light bulbs and screens, the sun and moon were the absolute rulers of our lives. We rose when the sun rose; we slept when the moon came out; we counted our days and months by watching these two celestial bodies cycle through the sky. Although we now have other means for tracking the passing hours, the sun and the moon still have the same level of influence over our internal journey as they have always had.

In astrology, we refer to the sun and the moon as "planets," which, of course, they are not. We designate them as planets not only because it simplifies things, but because they function basically like planets do in your chart. However, these two are like the parent planets—the sun is connected to masculine, fatherly energy, initiative, and ego, while the moon is connected to traditionally feminine and motherly energies, emotions, and nurturing. As you'll see throughout this section, the sun, the moon, and the astrological planets in general have historically been deeply intertwined with societal ideas about gender. The masculine sun is commanding; the feminine moon is receptive. The masculine Mars is aggressive; the feminine Venus is sensual, etc. At Sanctuary, we acknowledge this history *and*

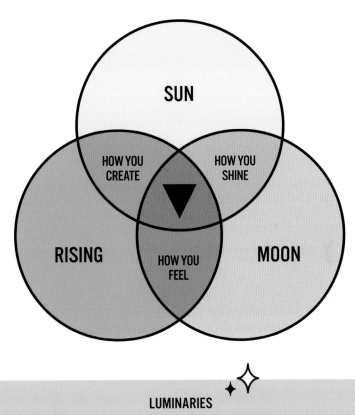

LUMINARIES

From the Latin word for "light," this is the name astrologers give to the sun and moon as they illuminate your chart. The luminaries shine their light on two of the basic sides of your personality and your karma. The sun illuminates your overarching self, and the moonlight reveals your inner world.

evolve beyond the limitations of traditional gender roles, and we acknowledge that these basic energies exist in all of us, no matter our individual gender. When we discuss the planetary personalities in gendered terms, we are talking about their traditional archetypes. Basically, we don't believe that men are from Mars and women are from Venus, but sometimes we'll still refer to their old school god/goddess roots for continuity!

And, since we're on the topic of evolving and diverse takes in astrology, a note on the luminaries of your chart: we're including your rising sign into the luminary category of your chart. Already considered the third part of the "Big Three" in astrology, your rising sign has just as much to say about how you show up in your life as the traditional sun and moon placements do. It's like that science class experiment where you shine different colored lights at the same spot on a wall and somehow those different colors all create a brilliant white light when they merge together. Together, the sun, moon, and rising signs illuminate your basic personality and are your entry point into a full astrological picture of who you are.

SUN

The sun is the home of your truest self. Just as the literal sun creates the conditions for life on Earth, the astrological sun is the source of creative energy in our charts. Our deepest inspirations and the highest dreams for our lives are both powered by the sun's energy. That's why astrologers often say that your sun sign is your ultimate identity, and why sun sign horoscopes are the most popular gateway into astrology. The placement of your sun reflects your overall approach to life, your values, and your creative energy.

However, it's a common oversimplification to say that your sun sign is "who you are." On the one hand, it's true that the basic energies of your sun sign are at the core of your psyche. All the other planets and the other aspects of your personality revolve around the sun. On the other hand, it makes sense that some people don't relate strongly to their sun sign because the seeds planted in the bedrock of your personality are not always immediately obvious, and they can be overshadowed by other planets and transits or by different situations in your life that might make other influences more prevalent. You're simply more complex than one sign, and that's totally normal!

IDENTITY:
HOW YOU SHINE

REPRESENTS
Your sense of self
Your primary concerns

SEE IT IN
Your life balance
Your instincts
What drives you

Instead of thinking of your sun sign as the last word in the story of who you are, think of it like the title of the book—and no matter what happens over the course of your life story, the sun stays central. To put it another way, the position of the sun in your chart is more a picture of who you are constantly becoming than who you appear to be at any given moment.

In astrology, the sun rules your highest self, the self that helps you choose who you are rather than reflecting who you are when you're on autopilot. The sun also shapes our ego and our will. The word "ego" often gets a bad rap, but don't think of it in the everyday sense of the word as in, "Oh, so-and-so has a huge ego." When we talk about the ego, we're talking about the part of ourselves that deals with reality, that steers the ship of our lives, and that makes compromises when necessary. Think of the sun as your inner parent, tempering the raw emotions of your inner child. The sun shapes the way you come to your final decisions, and in this way, it shapes the path of your life.

The sun guides us to the things that will feed our souls and also to the things that can fall out of whack in our lives if unhealthy patterns take root. When we work with the sun's influence in our charts, we are at our most energized, most focused, and most creative. However, any planet's influence can become a problem when its more challenging aspects take center stage. Say, for example, that your sun sign is Libra. When you're balanced and tuned in to this solar identity, you are the ultimate mediator, the sign that brings harmony to every situation. When the Libra tendency to give everyone what they want goes into overdrive, you might find yourself depleted and prone to white lies. But luckily for you, the way back to the blissful balance you crave is to use Libra's trademark eloquence to articulate boundaries and ask for what you need. That's the beauty of the sun! Even if you stray from the path, its light always guides you back.

Each planet rules at least one zodiac sign, and the sun rules only Leo. This makes total sense when you consider Leo's basic qualities: creativity, confidence, and that warm Leo affection. When a Leo is focused on you, it feels like there is a spotlight illuminating you both. The sun lends its fire to Leo and tends to drive

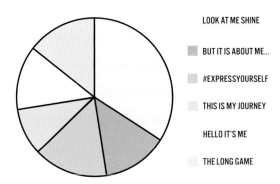

LOOK AT ME SHINE

BUT IT IS ABOUT ME...

#EXPRESSYOURSELF

THIS IS MY JOURNEY

HELLO IT'S ME

THE LONG GAME

people born under this sun sign into leadership roles and the spotlight. The challenging part of being ruled by the sun's immense energy is that it can be a lot of pressure! And solar lions may find themselves struggling with insecurity. The key for those ruled by the sun is to internalize the truth that they are enough, exactly as they are. There's no need to exaggerate or brag when you have the noble sun shining just for you.

Every year, there is a moment when the sun reaches the exact degree and minute it occupied when you were born. This is not only your birthday (yay!) but also your solar return. When the sun makes its return, that luminous influence that imbued your life with all of its grand potential is renewed. This is a time to take stock of your deepest motivations and your loftiest dreams and ask yourself if the life you're living feels fulfilling and authentic. If you spot some areas that need renovation, lean in to the strengths of your sun sign to help you plan your next chapter.

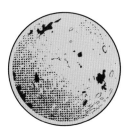

MOON

If the sun is the constant source of illumination and life-giving energy, the moon is a more mysterious presence. The light that the moon emanates is a glowing reflection of the sun. This glow illuminates our inner world, the watery realm of emotion, reaction, and our deepest needs. Although the sun's energy is powerful, it is also distant, always disappearing behind the horizon, always out of reach. The moon, on the other hand, is so intimately tied to our life on Earth

EMOTIONS:
HOW YOU REFLECT

REPRESENTS
Your emotional world
Your self-care

SEE IT IN
Your private thoughts
Your vulnerable moments
Your reactions to the world

that it can appear almost close enough to touch. The moon's presence in our skies ebbs and flows like the ocean tides that it creates in our seas. It's no wonder that, with all the moon's intrinsic ties to our life on Earth, astrologers pay special attention not just to the moon's position at the moment of our birth, but also its movement through the zodiac.

Astrologically, the moon represents the mother. We're not talking about your literal mom but more the archetype of maternal care and intimacy that is imprinted deep in our psyches, as well as the relationships we have to maternal figures (okay, sometimes we literally mean your mom). The moon indicates how we nurture ourselves and others, it can show us what we need in order to feel safe and comfortable, and it tells us about our reflexive patterns of behavior and underlying perspective on the world.

Care is not one-size-fits-all, and when it comes to self-care, many of us struggle to find out what works for us. Working with your moon sign can be a very powerful way to connect with the self-care practices that truly soothe you when you need it most. Diving into your moon sign's profile offers insight into how to cope after a hectic workday, after an emotionally draining argument, or in the throes of heartbreak or grief. When you feel totally depleted and vulnerable, the moon's imprint on your inner world becomes most obvious.

Have you ever tried to explain to someone what love means to you? If so, you've probably run up against the feeling that you can't really explain such deep experiences with words. This experience is like trying to tell someone about the part of you that the moon influences—the part that is so intimate that we struggle

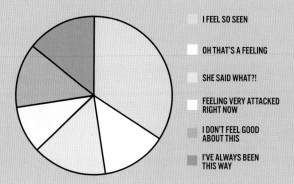

I FEEL SO SEEN

OH THAT'S A FEELING

SHE SAID WHAT?!

FEELING VERY ATTACKED
RIGHT NOW

I DON'T FEEL GOOD
ABOUT THIS

I'VE ALWAYS BEEN
THIS WAY

to explain why we react the way we do. We can only observe the influence in situations that draw these reactions out of us and allow those closest to us to witness us when we are truly vulnerable.

The moon rules only one sign: Cancer, the crab that lives in the liminal world of the tides, and it's pretty clear when you know a little about this celestial crab. Cancer is the most nurturing sign of the zodiac. Totally devoted to those they care about, they'll show their love to you by making sure that you always feel comfortable, safe, and at ease when you're with them. People born under a Cancer sun, moon, or with Cancer as their rising sign may come off as standoffish at times, and they can be hard to get close to. This is also an element of the moon's influence. Just as the moon plays a game of advance and retreat with the waves of the ocean, the moon shapes Cancers who are tentative about getting close to people. But this isn't because they are lacking in love or a desire for closeness—it's just the opposite. As the moon's subjects, Cancerians have boundless reserves of compassion and nurturing, but they need to feel safe in order to truly let people in.

Another testament to the moon's close ties to our lives is its monthly return to the point in the sky that it occupied at the moment of your birth. This, of course, is not an accident. The twelve months of our calendar year were originally based on the moon's cycle. Imagine how fun it would be if we were a society that counted lunar returns instead of solar returns. You wouldn't have to wait a whole year for your birthday—you'd get a party every month! Should we start a petition for moon days now or . . . ? Until the moon birthday becomes standard, you should know a few things about your lunar return and how to work with it.

When the moon makes its return in your chart, it reveals the emotional impact that the events of the coming month will have on you. If you're over the moon (ha ha) about lunar returns and you want to go deeper, you can start by looking at the ascendant or rising sign present when you generate an astrological chart for the timing of lunar return. This will tell you how your personality will manifest relative to your sun sign. You'll also want to pay attention to the aspects and angles of the chart. Or, you can just have an astrologer work out all the math-y bits and enjoy your monthly birthday.

RISING

The basic picture of who you are isn't complete without your rising sign. Your whole birth chart begins with the rising sign, or the sign that rose in the eastern horizon in the sky when you were born. Your rising sign is the line between the twelfth house in your chart and the first house, and this changes every two hours (which is why precise birth info is so important!). Also called your ascendant sign, this part of your chart reveals the impressions you make on others. This placement determines the version of "you" that is projected to others; it sets the tone for how you see the world and how you interact within your surroundings. If you're not totally sold on your sun sign as an accurate representation of who you are, you're not alone. Many of us are more in touch with our rising sign because it's the version of who we are that is most often reinforced by the people around us and the experiences of our day-to-day lives.

OUTWARD PERSONA: HOW YOU ACT

REPRESENTS
Your perspective
Your decisions

SEE IT IN
Your style
Your embellishments
Your daily choices

Together with your sun and moon sign, the sign that was rising as you were born creates a general picture of who you are, while the other placements in your chart depict more nuanced aspects of your personality and your life. You might have noticed that, unlike the other two key players (the sun and moon), your rising sign is not an astrological planet. The rising sign is not a planet or a zodiac sign, instead it is the cusp of your first house. The reason this spot carries so much astrological weight is that it serves as a kind of starting place for all the other energies in your natal chart, including your sun and moon. Because this sign is so specific to the time and place of your birth, it captures the early environment and the social conditioning that shapes the way all the other placements manifest in your interactions. It is an imprint of the energetic gateway that you pass through as you are born. The rising sign is sometimes called the mask you wear for other people. This isn't to say that we're all hiding who we really are—it's just the way we were formed on the surface, and it's as true to who we are as any of the other natal influences, especially in childhood when so much is projected onto us. Some astrologers believe that the rising sign takes more of a backseat in our personalities as we age, get more comfortable in our own skin, and grow into our unique destiny.

The rising sign has a lot to do with sight—it is the first sign we see on the horizon, and it is the first way people see us. It impacts our first impressions, and

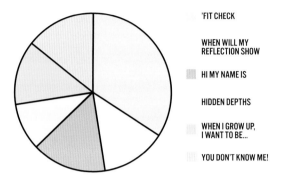

'FIT CHECK

WHEN WILL MY
REFLECTION SHOW

HI MY NAME IS

HIDDEN DEPTHS

WHEN I GROW UP,
I WANT TO BE...

YOU DON'T KNOW ME!

many astrologers think that it even shapes our physical appearance and elements of our health. For example, Libra rising folks are said to have melodic voices, big smiles, and great personal style, whereas Leo rising people might have a distinct mane of hair, dramatic facial expressions, and a regal bearing. Of course, these traits are subjective and vary dramatically across cultures and times. But astrology is most useful when it is understood as a creative and interpretive art *based* on astronomical science. The insights gained from learning about your rising sign are meant to be reflective, intuitive, and generative instead of precise and perfectly literal.

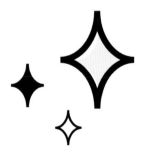

THE PERSONAL PLANETS

MERCURY	VENUS	MARS
"I THINK"	"I WANT"	"I ACT"
CONNECTION	LOVE	MOTIVATION
SPEECH	DESIRES	PURSUITS
LEARNS	ADORES	REACTS
THOUGHT	PLEASURE	STRENGTH
☿	♀	♂

Although the sun, moon, and rising sign get the most airtime, the placement of Venus, Mars, and Mercury in your birth chart have a lot to say about who you are. These personal planets, also called "the inner planets," orbit closest to the Earth and represent the major aspects of our personalities—our minds, hearts, and how we get the things we want in life. Understanding the personal planets is the next stop on your grand tour of astrological power players.

These placements may not get as much publicity as the sun, moon, and rising signs, but the personal planets offer us insight into the hot topics and useful snippets that we all love in our horoscopes. These are the actors on the stage of our psyche, and they each play their own role. When we want to know about our love lives, we check out Venus; for real talk about how we exert our will, we hit Mars up; and Mercury is our go-to for insight into the way our minds work.

Unlike the planets farther away in the galaxy, the personal planets are intimately tied to our day-to-day lives. Their transits, retrogrades, and returns are all tangled up in the energetic currents of our lives. We feel their changing moods and behaviors in part because their orbits make more immediate sense within our lifetimes. The far-out planets move so slowly that their energies are dispersed over whole generations of people, rather than the specific, emotional sensation of our Venus, Mars, and Mercury placements. But we'll get to the outer planets a little later. For now, you just need to know that the movements of these three planets help shape our day-to-day experiences in society and our internal moods and motivations.

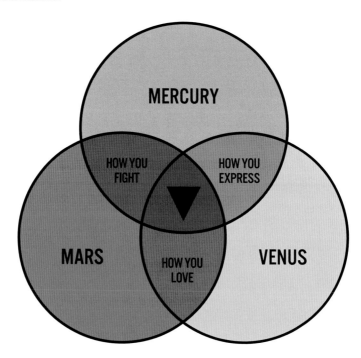

VENUS

Named after the Roman goddess of love and beauty, the astrological Venus fittingly presides over the most romantic and sensual domains of our lives. But Venus influences way more than which emoji you're most likely to send your crush. The love planet's goddess namesake was thought of as the archetypal artist and lover. To the ancient Romans, she represented all that is indulgent and delicious about the human experience. Depending on the planets Venus interacts with, this planetary influence can be lovingly compassionate or excessively hedonistic. It's a planet that points out what you value with your money, time, and energy. Venus energy also manifests in the way that we seek pleasure, pampering, and money. Venus's energy is feminine, but not in the same way as the moon. Where the moon's take

PERSONAL PLANETS

The planets closest to the sun including Mars, Venus, and Mercury are called "the personal planets" because their impacts are more readily felt in our lives. The luminaries (sun and moon) are also sometimes considered personal planets. All of these together form the basic energies of our charts, and their influence in our lives depends on where (which house) these planets are in. Because these planets move quickly and change signs often, they create a lot of variation in birth charts, even in people born a few days (or hours) apart!

ATTRACTION:
HOW YOU FEEL

REPRESENTS
Your values
Your desires

SEE IT IN
Your crushes
Your bank account
Your shopping list

on femininity is about security and nurturing, Venus's femininity is all about seduction, charm, and attraction. No matter your gender or your belief about your own ability to charm people's socks off, Venus's influence is present in your psychological makeup, and when you learn to work with this energy, you find a deep reserve of power and confidence. To illustrate all the ways Venusian energy influences our lives, let's consider the zodiac signs that Venus rules.

The planet of love and pleasure prefers to be spoiled, so of course Venus isn't satisfied with ruling just one sign. Venus is in charge of both Taurus and Libra, and learning about these two signs can tell us about the different ways that its energy can manifest. Taurus, the earthy bull, might not seem like the most obvious pick for team Venus at first glance. But make no mistake, you'll never meet a more sensual sign. Venus shapes Taurus's affinity for all the physical manifestations of luxury and pleasure. Taurus loves to be pampered and showered with rewards for their hard work. They want to be wined and dined and romanced—sound like anyone you know? Ahem, hello, Venus! Then, we have sophisticated air sign Libra. Libra is represented by the scales, always seeking to bring things into a state of equilibrium. Libran energy is all about justice and getting it in the politest way possible. Libra gets their love of harmony, their charm, and their refined taste from Venus.

The challenging side of Venus's energy can take her love of beauty and twist it into vanity—or if threatened, all that charm can become manipulative. One common way that Venus's challenging energy can manifest in both the signs that it rules has to do with the way that both these signs make decisions. Where stubborn Taurus might tend to get stuck in their comfort zone, airy Libra might struggle to make a decision because they get bogged down in deliberation. To put it in the form of a math class word problem: Two signs walk into a corner store to buy a snack. Taurus chooses the same corner store and buys the same bag of chips every day, even if they secretly want to expand their horizons. Libra walks into whichever corner store has the prettiest window display and can't decide which chips they want, or if maybe they should get an ice cream instead, so they just walk out with nothing. Which of these two signs is a wayward child of Venus? Answer: yep. It's both of 'em.

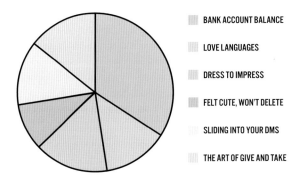

- BANK ACCOUNT BALANCE
- LOVE LANGUAGES
- DRESS TO IMPRESS
- FELT CUTE, WON'T DELETE
- SLIDING INTO YOUR DMS
- THE ART OF GIVE AND TAKE

Venus stays close to us even as she roams along her orbit. As an inner planet, Venus takes four to five weeks to transit a single sign and goes retrograde every eighteen months. The astrological lover makes sure to stop in and make a grand return to the same point in the sky it occupied at your birth roughly once every year. Your Venus return is a bubbly time that calls for celebration, delight, and all the finer things. You'll notice a sparkle in your eyes and a playful energy that tempts you to skip school, call in sick, and spend all day shopping for luxury bath products or setting up a big date.

Speaking of big dates, your Venus return doesn't have to involve literal romantic intrigue, but Venus loves love, and if you *are* looking to spark up something new, this is a good time to ask that cutie you always see in the elevator for their number. Although Venus loves to make a scene, its annual return might not pack quite the wallop that, say, Saturn does with its twenty-nine-year orbit, because it's only been a year since Venus showed up last! Planetary returns are all about the cycles of growth and the transformation of energy, and in astrological time, a year isn't that long. Nonetheless, Venus doesn't like to be ignored, and a great way to celebrate its annual return is to spend some time pampering yourself and getting in touch with your sensuality in whatever way feels the most titillating!

MARS

Named after the god of war, Mars is the planet of our physicality, our style of aggression, and our sexuality. Traditionally, Mars is thought of as embodying the masculine energy present in all of our lives. This is the energy of momentum, the energy that it takes to break out of inertia and create new things. When you're lying in bed, feeling aimless and lacking motivation, it's Mars you need to look for. The placement of Mars in your chart indicates the nature of your drive and your overall temperament. Mars determines whether you're more likely to flip a table in the heat of an argument or order another round to smooth over the conflict. Your Mars placement also tells you about what gets you hot and bothered, what turns your head—basically, it tells you which kind of thirst traps are most likely to get you to send an impulsive DM. When Mars energy gets carried away in your life, you might have a shorter fuse than usual, and maybe that rage text you sent in response to one of those auto-generated spam messages was a little harsh and also ineffective because robots know no shame. It's okay, though! Learning more about Martian energy is the best way to recognize when you might be burning a bit too brightly and how to redirect that energy to productive ends.

♂

ACTION:
HOW YOU FIGHT

REPRESENTS
Your determination
Your passion

SEE IT IN
Your drive
Your scorecard
Your hormones

Mars asks us to be honest about what sparks our passion—where in your life are you courageous, and where are you more timid? What makes you get up and go in the morning? How do you chase the things you want? Depending on where Mars is placed in your chart, the way you express your inner fire can vary in big ways. For example, let's say your Mars is in dreamy Pisces. This placement is all about passion that comes from the heart, and you are most fired up when you're standing up for the underdogs. Or, say your Mars is in Scorpio. The sexuality of a Mars in Scorpio is deeply tied to emotional connection. This placement shapes people who are ultimate comeback kids. They are persistent, resilient, and unafraid of conflict. Mars amplifies Scorpio's inherent drive and, like a phoenix rising from the ashes, the superpower for this placement is that they never give up. No matter how many times they get knocked down, they won't stay down for long. Sensually magnetic and passionate, people with their Mars in Scorpio radiate powerful sex appeal and are fiercely loyal. Same planet, different placements, totally different vibes.

Let's talk more about this relationship between Mars and its favorite sign, Aries, the fiery ram that initiates a whole new cycle in the astrological calendar (after all, it kicks off spring in the northern hemisphere!). Mars's fingerprints are all over some of Aries's best-known characteristics. When it comes to Aries, you can see Mars's high energy and that signature quick temper. As the first sign of the zodiac, Aries is all about starting new things and they get that unstoppable momentum from Mars. Aries is also known for telling things straight. The celestial ram does not sugarcoat the truth, and they don't mind if they step on some toes in the process. If Mars's influence gets out of hand in Aries's life, it can make them a magnet for conflict. But when Aries works to become intentional and focuses their passion, all that fire is a Martian gift!

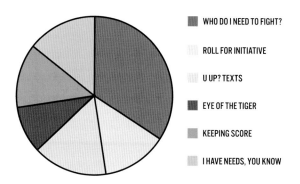

- WHO DO I NEED TO FIGHT?
- ROLL FOR INITIATIVE
- U UP? TEXTS
- EYE OF THE TIGER
- KEEPING SCORE
- I HAVE NEEDS, YOU KNOW

When Mars makes its way back to the same point in the sky that it occupied at the moment of your birth, you've got yourself a Mars return, baby! Every two years, you and Mars sit down for a quick review of how you've been spending your energy and how you should spend that energy over the next two years. Remember, this planet not only rules your literal temper—it also indicates how you solve problems, the nature of your willpower, your self-discipline, and how you assert yourself. Looking at your Mars return chart can tell you about whether the next cycle will be a time of constant power struggles or a time where everything seems to go your way. It can tell you about which battles are worth fighting and which hills aren't worth dying on. Some people do whatever they can to avoid learning the lessons of Mars. We see so many unhealthy expressions of will and power all around us that we may turn away from our own power out of fear that we might wield it in a way that harms others or makes us unlikable. Some people lean on their inner fighter too much and walk around with a chip on their shoulder to mask a fearful or wounded heart. Neither of these paths honors the powerful and potentially productive influence of Mars. On the occasion of your Mars return, pay attention to the house that this planet falls in. Whatever area of your life is impacted by that house will serve as your laboratory for the next two years. In this laboratory, you will practice using Mars's energy in a responsible and self-respecting way. No need to puff up, no need to shrink down—take a deep breath and stand your ground.

MERCURY

Mercury rules our minds, our intellectual proclivities, and the way we communicate—so you know that this planet has *a lot to say* when it comes to your personality! We hate that pun, too, but Mercury loves wordplay, so sorry, not sorry—call Mercury with your complaints. Speaking of phone calls, Mercury is all about 'em! And texts, and emails, and literally all the things we use to communicate with each other, which is why Mercury retrograde gets so much hate (but

COMMUNICATION: HOW YOU THINK

REPRESENTS
Your mind
Your speech

SEE IT IN
Your texting speed
Your notifications
Your problem solving

we'll get to that in a sec). Normally, the communication planet keeps things moving along and determines how you express yourself and interpret the information you take in from the world around you. When working with other planets, Mercury's logical and rational position helps to frame your emotions, actions, and romantic life.

Contrary to popular belief, Mercury is more than an on/off switch that controls whether we actually sent that important email or whether it somehow ended up in the drafts folder. Because your Mercury placement indicates how you go about your day-to-day communications, people tend to encounter your Mercury first in our high-tech world. This is the planet that impacts how you email, text, and all the ways you connect at a distance. The placement of Mercury in your chart also tells you about your analytical mind, or how you apply logic and rationality in your life.

This is also the placement that indicates how you process information, how you share your ideas with the world, and what topics you're drawn to learning about. Are you a fast-talking storyteller who loves a tangent? Are you the kind of person that takes your time when learning something new, but once you get it, you've got it for good? Do you land your words, or are you more reserved? Mercury's placement in your chart is the place to look if you're trying to find some answers!

With all that in its sphere of influence, it's no wonder Mercury wreaks havoc when it reverses course. And that's why this planet has a bit of a reputation problem. When we're stressed or stretched thin, or when Mercury moves through a challenging angle in its progress through the sky, we can become nervous,

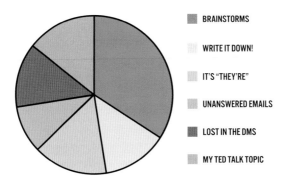

BRAINSTORMS

WRITE IT DOWN!

IT'S "THEY'RE"

UNANSWERED EMAILS

LOST IN THE DMS

MY TED TALK TOPIC

high-strung, and overly critical. When this naughty planet goes retrograde, all the normal Mercury stuff like timing, tech, and communication in general goes haywire. Expect travel delays, technology meltdowns, misinterpretation, and frustrating miscommunication. Be aware of any upcoming Mercury retrogrades and prepare yourself by backing up your data, planning extra time for travel, and making sure you choose your words wisely.

Looking at key qualities of the signs that a given planet rules grants us a practical understanding of the planet's influence in our lives. In Mercury's case, Gemini and Virgo amplify different aspects of their ruling planet's energy. Virgo is the sign that strives for perfection, but not the perfection that a more whimsical sign might find in a decadent meal (looking at you, Taurus) or the perfect pair of gorgeous but completely impractical platforms (hi, Libra!). Virgo's version of perfection is definitely shaped by Mercury's focus on objective analysis. Virgo loves to analyze systems, tackle complex problems, and make efficient progress toward their goals. Virgo embodies Mercury's love of knowledge and logic, but not so much the chatty side of the communication planet. Virgo shines when they're able to absorb, process, and synthesize new information.

To get a glimpse of Mercury's influence in full social-butterfly mode, look to Gemini. Where earth sign Virgo is all about the practical applications of analysis,

Gemini shines by making quick and surprising connections and sharing those connections with other people. When we say other people, we mean literally everyone—because if there's one thing a Gemini loves, it's conversation. Mercury's energy manifests in Gemini's embrace of connection, their lightning-fast mind, and their gift of gab. Gemini can out-small talk any sign in the zodiac, but it's not because they're superficial. Gemini rocks at small talk because Mercury gave the celestial twins a lively energy and a deep curiosity about the world around them that rivals any other sign in the zodiac. They might lack Virgo's neat, objective talent for putting everything in its proper place, but they make up for it with their creativity and the ability to bring people together. You'll also want to look into which house your natal Mercury appears, as this can tell you which areas of your life you tend to focus on intellectually, or the area of your life where you need to express yourself in order to feel fulfilled.

Mercury takes about two weeks to move through, or transit, a single sign, and it goes retrograde three to four times per year, making its return to the precise sign and degree that it occupied when you first popped into the world occur every year right around your birthday! Like all planetary returns, Mercury's return is a moment when one cycle or pattern ends in your life and another one begins, simultaneously. In Mercury's case, this planetary return tells you which patterns of communication or modes of expression might be prevalent in the coming cycle of its movement. This return shows us where our mental energy will be focused and what obstacles to understanding and being understood may arise.

GENERATIONAL PLANETS

JUPITER	SATURN	URANUS	NEPTUNE	PLUTO
"I GROW"	"I CONTROL"	"I CHANGE"	"I DREAM"	"I DECONSTRUCT"
EXPANSION	STRUCTURE	UPHEAVAL	ILLUSIONS	TRANSFORMATION
PHILOSOPHY	ROUTINES	INNOVATION	SPIRITUALITY	ANCESTRY
HOPES	COMMANDS	REVOLTS	VISUALIZES	BREAKS
LUCK	ORDER	PROGRESS	DREAMS	ALCHEMY
♃	♄	♅	♆	♇

While the inner planets shape our immediate, personal experiences, we have powerful players shaping the tides of our collective experience. Jupiter, Uranus, Neptune, and Pluto have a big-picture perspective and their energies elevate our awareness. These planets ask us to transcend the purely personal and tap into energy that exceeds our individual identity. They bring luck, religion, philosophy, destruction, dreams, and enlightenment.

These planets take a long time to complete their orbits—like, we're talking 165 years in Neptune's case. This means that they take their time transiting the signs of the zodiac, so everyone born during the multi-year period that it takes one of these planets to move through a sign shares that sign for that planet. In this way, these outer planets shape whole swaths of people born in the same generation into distinct cohorts with passions, beliefs, and tastes that diverge from

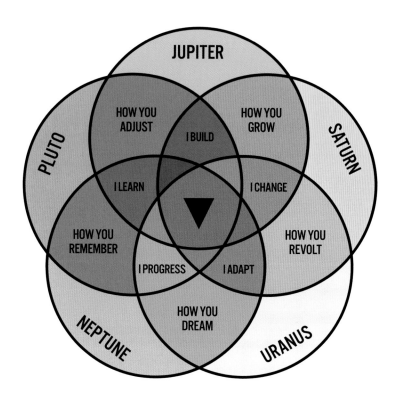

GENERATIONAL PLANETS

Uranus, Neptune, and Pluto are called "the generational planets" or "the outer planets" interchangeably, and this latter name gives us a pretty good hint as to why! These planets are farthest away from the Earth and have longer cycles of orbit. This means that their influence is felt less in your personal life and more as general themes over the course of your life. You're likely to share these with people born around the same year or even a few years, hence the "generational" moniker.

the generations before and after them. We know and feel this impact intuitively when we relate to people born in our celestial cohort. One way to look at this is to look at the differences between you and your friends' beliefs and lifestyles and those of your parents' generation. It's common knowledge that parents and children sometimes struggle to speak the same language, and a lot of that has to do with the generational difference of outer planet placements.

While the specific placement of these planets in your natal chart (as in, the house they fall in and the aspects they form with other planets) can definitely offer insight about where in your life you interact with that planet's energy and how you go about it, their fundamental influence is shared in the community.

JUPITER

Jupiter is in charge of our abstract mind and bestows us all with the urge to explore (specific to the sign it occupies in our chart, of course). Jupiter is all about a search for answers, and its planetary energy shapes the things we believe to be true and good. This is the planet of abundance, luck, expansion, and the good old-fashioned experience of laughing so hard you cry. That latter part of Jupiter's personality, about humor and play, gets less attention than its reputation for good luck and for trying to figure out the meaning of life. But don't sleep on Jupiter's love of leisure! This connection between abundance and rest is a key lesson for all of us about the importance of balancing hard work with warm naps in the sun. When Jupiter isn't busy arm wrestling Saturn and playing hide and seek with Earth, it gets to work

♃

EXPANSION:
HOW YOU GROW

REPRESENTS
Your optimistic outlook
Your vices

SEE IT IN
Your lucky charms
Your wild side
Your sense of humor

bringing good fortune into our lives. Jupiter's placement in your chart shows you which areas of your life you're likely to be especially lucky in, which doors will open for you most easily, and what comes naturally to you.

The Roman god Jupiter that lends this planet its name was the most highly exalted god in ancient Roman culture. Jupiter was lord of the sky, the god who granted auspicious wishes and represented faith and wisdom. In astrology, we retain a lot of qualities associated with the OJ (Original Jupiter). We look at Jupiter in our charts to give us insight into our own predilections and modes of operation in the realm of religion, ideology, higher education, philosophy, and prosperity.

As an actual planet, Jupiter is the biggest kid on the block, dwarfing puny Mercury and the other personal planets. And not only does Jupiter's literal size align with the planet's energy of expansion and abundance, it also indicates to us that Jupiter will have a role in how we handle some of the bigger questions in life: What do you truly believe in? How open-minded are you to differences? Where in your life are you showing up as extreme or excessive? Jupiter's placement in your chart also shows us how we extend our generosity, how we feel about trusting other people, and how we go about making positive changes in our lives. For example, say that your natal Jupiter is in hardworking, tradition-loving Capricorn. This placement indicates that you have tons of discipline in your work, strong bonds with your family, and likely will succeed in a career like politics or government work. The challenging part of this placement is that it could make you a little too conservative or closed-minded, lacking tolerance for the more eccentric people and ideas you encounter. Or, say your natal Jupiter is in spotlight-loving Leo. This placement suggests confidence and deeply rooted optimism. In terms of wealth and success, your generosity is unparalleled, and because you view the world as an endlessly abundant place, you have no problem sharing with others. The challenging side of this placement is the risk of egotism and a tendency to take big risks when you shouldn't.

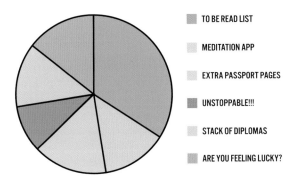

- TO BE READ LIST
- MEDITATION APP
- EXTRA PASSPORT PAGES
- UNSTOPPABLE!!!
- STACK OF DIPLOMAS
- ARE YOU FEELING LUCKY?

Jupiter rules Sagittarius, the zodiac's intrepid archer. This sign is all about the quest for knowledge and understanding. This sign finds it hard to sit still and is always chasing adventure, both in terms of literal travel and exploration and in spiritual and intellectual pursuits. Sag is an eternal optimist, quick to laugh and always at the ready with a dazzling story taken from one of their many exploits. Jupiter's influence is clear when we look at these well-known Sag qualities. Jupiter's energy of abundance and expansion is at the root of Sag's unrelenting drive to discover new places, people, and ideas, as well as their inclination to spread that knowledge around. When Jupiter's energy takes a negative turn, this can signal a change of fortune, or perhaps that you've moved from charming storyteller with a captive audience to big-time know-it-all with an audience looking for an excuse to make an exit. Just like every planet or sign in the zodiac, the energy of Jupiter can be harnessed to amazing ends, but left unchecked, it can be a little much for people.

Jupiter makes its return to the same spot it occupied when you were born only once every twelve years. This is definitely a cause for celebration, as Jupiter brings all its big luck and abundant energy to the party. "Big" is really the operative word here, because a major theme of this return is expansion. This is a time where you'll find yourself thinking bigger, seeing the big picture, and chasing bigger dreams than you had during the last twelve-year cycle. A cautionary word on Jupiter's return: check in with yourself about that ego of yours during the early days of a new Jupiter cycle, because that expansive energy can become a bit of a problem when the part of you that expands too much is your ego. But, hey, it's Jupiter we're talking about, so let's finish on an optimistic note. Because Jupiter is the anything-is-possible planet, your Jupiter return is the perfect time to take action on that pie-in-the-sky idea that's been kicking around in your head for a while now. So on the grand occasion of your Jupiter return, make sure to capitalize on all that positivity, optimism, and vision.

SATURN

Saturn is sometimes called "the lord of time," and it rules how you spend it, where you dedicate it, and what you do with it. This discerning planet defines our limits and indicates where we'll be met with obstacles in our life. And, although Saturn is known as a bit of a taskmaster, this planet never asks you to overcome something just to put you through the ringer. Saturn promises that if you rise to meet the occasion, you will be better for it. A more holistic understanding of Saturn recognizes that limitations and boundaries are necessary in order to define your sense of self.

ħ

STRUCTURE:
HOW YOU CONTRACT

REPRESENTS
Your discipline
Your well-being

SEE IT IN
Your routine
Your better sense
Your five-year plan

As you grow over the course of Saturn's twenty-nine(ish)-year cycle, you'll distinguish yourself from the people around you by learning to say "no" to the things that don't serve you. Saturn is the force that pushes our evolution, day by day, as we become who we are. When Saturn is doing its job, this planet keeps us on track and keeps us from getting blown off course or wandering too far away from who we truly are. Yes, at times Saturn can undermine our grand designs or force us to let go of habits and beliefs that we are attached to, sometimes for our own good. Saturn is the necessary force in our life to define and clarify our identity and our growth areas. None of the big dreams and lofty aspirations that other astrological bodies incite can come to fruition without determination, discernment, and concentration.

Saturn rules Capricorn, the hardest-working sea-goat in the sky. Capricorn is all about mastery. You might think that this constellation with the body of a goat and the tail of a fish is a strange and delightful mashup of creatures that the ancient Romans made up for funsies, which, sure, is probably half true. But this creature also represents astrological Capricorn's drive to dexterously navigate both the material and emotional realms. And with tough-love Saturn as their ruling planet, Capricorn is no stranger to trials by fire. In fact, many Caps go through significant challenges early on in life, which has Saturn written all over it.

Luckily, the time lord is not just out there bullying baby sea-goats for fun. People say Capricorns age in reverse, becoming more and more playful and open-hearted as they get older. Cap also gets their deep respect for customs and family values from traditional Saturn. What does this planet's super grown-up, no-nonsense influence look like in signs that are a little less on the straight and narrow? Let's look at Saturn in Cancer, a sign with many of the opposite qualities of Saturn's chosen sea-goat.

When Saturn lands in Cancer on your natal chart, you've got all of Saturn's tendency to push people toward duty and responsibility mixed with Cancer's inherent need to nurture others, adding up to the ultimate giver. People with this placement take domestic matters extremely seriously. Saturn in this placement amplifies Cancer's tendency to keep their emotions and their vulnerabilities under wraps. They probably learned to take on the responsibilities earlier on in life or were told they were too sensitive. This shapes resilient people with soft hearts and hard shells. Their big Saturn challenge? Learning to put themselves first sometimes, and to keep their heart open to new experiences and relationships. Saturn is all about discernment, remember?

No matter where your natal Saturn falls in the zodiac, the planet of responsibility makes its way back to the same spot every twenty-nine years or so. Saturn's

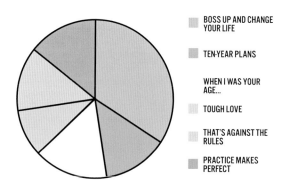

BOSS UP AND CHANGE YOUR LIFE

TEN-YEAR PLANS

WHEN I WAS YOUR AGE...

TOUGH LOVE

THAT'S AGAINST THE RULES

PRACTICE MAKES PERFECT

return is probably the most well-known return these days after your solar return, and for good reason. With such a long orbit, this planet packs a major punch because it had so much time to develop its energy in your life. Another reason this return gets a lot of airtime is that even if you're not an astrology buff, everyone knows that the last few years of your twenties are a time when many people start to think of themselves differently, maybe even feeling a little bit—gasp—grown-up!

Before Saturn returns in your birth chart, it might seem like you have infinite time to decide who you want to be when you grow up. But as we get closer to the big three-zero, we are asked to commit to a path and to let the things that don't align with our true selves go. Exhibit A: According to the US census, there is a peak in divorce for people around the age of thirty when commitments we might have made in our early adulthood no longer sync up with the person we've become or the person we're meant to be. But on the bright side, most people in the US also get married between the ages of twenty-five and thirty, so there's that. The statistics go on and on, and the trend is pretty consistent: this is a time where you decide what kind of grown-up you want to be, and this can be a really scary thing to consider!

Fear not, because every Saturn return (and we're lucky to get two or even three if we make it to our nineties) is an opportunity to find out what kind of butterfly you've been transforming into within your thirty-year chrysalis, and your natal Saturn placement provides you with a blueprint. If you've made it through your first Saturn return, congratulations! Even if you don't feel like you've figured out exactly who you are just yet, don't worry—you have plenty of time to work on it. If your big return is still on the horizon, look at your natal Saturn placement to find out where you need to cultivate some grit.

URANUS

Surprise! It's time to talk about the planet that tells us to expect the unexpected. Uranus is the great innovator, always looking to shake things up and remind us that the only constant in life is change. This planet always has its eyes trained on the future and is not interested in the conventional ways of doing things. This energy is all about innovation, technology, and breaking down systems in order to make space for new possibilities. Uranus is not interested in causing chaos just for the sake of chaos, this disruption is a necessary part of progress, and enlightenment is never the result of things just plodding along, business as usual. This is the planet of fierce independence, and sometimes this planet pops in to jolt us from a dream-like state of following the leader or going along with society's expectations, and it can wake us up to our own self-determination.

When we connect with Uranus, our intuition suddenly becomes electric and vivid. We start to see new pathways where we thought there were only dead ends. The energy of Uranus is kind of like Mercury, the ruler of our intellectual mind—if Mercury got all hopped-up on caffeine and started having eureka moments every five minutes. Where Mercury would carefully weigh out all its options before making a move, Uranus likes to move fast and break things without stopping to second-guess its impulses.

For such a rebellious planet, Uranus moves relatively slowly around the sun, taking eighty-four years to complete a full orbit and about seven years to move through a single sign. This means that everyone born within a seven-year period will have the same Uranus sign. In modern astrology, people tend to overlook Uranus because it has less to say about an individual's personality than it does about the trajectory and spirit of your generation. For example, if you were born between the years of 1988 and 1996, your Uranus sign is Capricorn. The Uranus in Capricorn generation takes Capricorn's focus on tradition and turns it on its head. This is a generation that looks at outmoded systems, governments, and expectations and seeks to dismantle them. These folks are not interested in band-aids for what is broken in our society. They want to take the old

**INNOVATION:
HOW YOU REVOLT**

REPRESENTS
Your innovation
Your rebellion

SEE IT IN
Your righteous anger
Your revelations
Your ideas for a better world

ways of doing things that served only the most powerful among us and replace them with innovative and technologically advanced models that are based in integrity and authenticity.

It makes sense, of course, that this unconventional planet would rule eccentric Aquarius, the humanistic sign that pursues innovative solutions for humanity's biggest problems. Uranus crashes through the limitations and the crystalized sense of self that Saturn cultivates and displaces all the systems and beliefs that no longer serve us as a society. This influence is clear in Aquarius, the water bearer who will do whatever it takes to end oppression and injustice wherever it exists. Just as Uranus revels in the unpredictable, Aquarius tends to shock more conservative types with their far-out ideas. Although Uranus most clearly electrifies Aquarius and gives this sign its fundamental energy and orientation, we all feel the influence of Uranus. That sudden bolt of insight, the revelation, the inspiration that strikes us when we least expect it—this is Uranus making itself known.

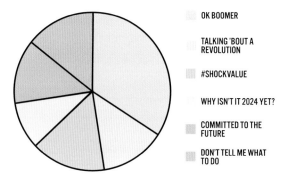

OK BOOMER

TALKING 'BOUT A
REVOLUTION

#SHOCK VALUE

WHY ISN'T IT 2024 YET?

COMMITTED TO THE
FUTURE

DON'T TELL ME WHAT
TO DO

Because of Uranus's drawn-out orbit, this planet takes about eighty-four years to move through all twelve signs of the zodiac and arrive back to its original position in your natal chart. If we're lucky enough to make it to this stage of our lives, we'll be primed for an amazing breakthrough. When Uranus returns to its natal home, the lucky octogenarian encounters the possibility of completely throwing off the last restraints of societal expectation and conventional beliefs. This is a moment in life where the hard work of living a long life is rewarded by Uranus, who struts in like a long-lost friend to say: Are you ready to be exactly, brilliantly who you are? Are you ready to see what life is like when you finally stop caring about what the world thinks you ought to be?

NEPTUNE

Named for the god of the sea, Neptune rules over the domain of our deep sub-conscious, as well as our spiritual and psychic experiences. Neptune is the planet in charge of dreams and all the murky, buried meanings, the mystic inspiration, and the illusions that come with them. Neptune rules all the subtle energies of our lives, especially our spirituality. Neptune's influence on our spiritual life is not like Jupiter's abstract conceptions of religion and philosophy. According to Jupiter, the answers are out there, and in order to find them, we must tirelessly seek out education and experiences that will refine our thinking over time. According to Neptune, spirituality is an embodied experience and requires us to be still and look inward, rather than chasing the meaning of life. This is the planet of spiritual experience and healing. It helps us connect with the unseen layers of life and to dissolve all the boundaries between the ego and the world, drawing us into a sense

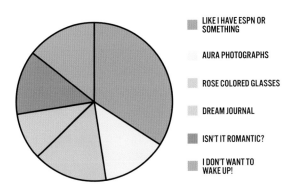

LIKE I HAVE ESPN OR SOMETHING

AURA PHOTOGRAPHS

ROSE COLORED GLASSES

DREAM JOURNAL

ISN'T IT ROMANTIC?

I DON'T WANT TO WAKE UP!

**SPIRITUALITY:
HOW YOU DREAM**

REPRESENTS
Your fantasies
Your imagination

SEE IT IN
Your reality checks
Your daydreams
Your spirituality

of sublime oneness. Neptune is sensitive, gentle, and loving. Where Venus (the planet that rules romantic love) is focused on value, partnership, and attraction, Neptune represents universal love and compassion, a vast, loving presence encompassing all beings.

Neptune rules Pisces, the dreamiest sign in the zodiac. This is a sign that always has one fin in reality and one fin in the watery realm of intuition. Pisces is the last sign of the zodiac, wrapping up a full cycle of growth—meaning that the cosmic fish has learned all the lessons of the signs that came before it. The psychic capacities that Pisces is known for are drawn from all the wisdom, joy, and sorrow of the other eleven signs accumulated into deep Piscean insight. The very heart of Pisces's experience is colored by intuition, imagination, and dreams. This is the influence of Neptune, always calling Pisces to new depths of psychic sensitivity.

In your natal chart, Neptune's placement can point to how you develop your psychic powers, your creativity, and your intuition. On a bad day, Neptune's placement in your natal chart exposes your blind spots. This is Neptune playing the trickster, the master of illusion. In this case, Neptune points out the areas of life we romanticize, idealize, or refuse to acknowledge.

Neptune is never in a rush and doesn't move according to human schedules. This planet takes 168 years—well over a human lifetime—to make its natal return. That doesn't mean we don't feel Neptune's presence. Since Neptune takes thirteen to fourteen years to transit a single sign, we feel its impact generationally and collectively. Because of Neptune's dominion over the subtle and subconscious mind, its transits often reveal cultural shifts and movements within the arts. Overall, Neptune's influence is most observable when looking at the tides of history and the spirit of the present moment.

PLUTO

Doing its own thing far in the outer reaches of our galaxy, Pluto is the ruler of the underworld. The planet farthest beyond our reach rules the unseen forces that drive transformation. Pluto is the force that helps us achieve the highest levels of spiritual awakening, although this process is never fast, cheap, or easy. This is the planet that governs secrets and undercover information, so its placement reveals the areas of life that require deep dives into the soul. Pluto's presence in your natal chart exposes the areas in your life that will require total and complete transformation.

As the modern ruler of Scorpio, Pluto is the influence that lies beneath that infamous Scorpio intensity. Understanding Scorpio's driving motivations and qualities is a good way to get to know distant Pluto. Scorpio's energy is drawn to the shadowy side of life. This urge is not the result of morbid curiosity. Scorpio is magnetized to the experiences that most others would turn away from because the primary drives in Scorpio's life are transformation, birth, and rebirth (and all the steps in-between). Scorpio, like the planet that rules it, is a kind of alchemist, taking poison and transmuting it into medicine. Pluto and Scorpio are both deeply powerful, and they represent a kind of healing that only comes from confronting

TRANSFORMATION: HOW YOU LET GO

REPRESENTS
Your rebirth
Your power

SEE IT IN
Your baggage
Your journey
What you let go

the darkest experiences in life and making it through to the other side.

Pluto takes its time moving across the sky. It takes this generational planet twelve to thirty years to move through a single sign and 248 years to make it all the way through the zodiac! This means that you share your Pluto sign with your generation. Most millennials, for example, have Pluto in Scorpio. This has shaped a generation of willful, passionate revolutionaries hell-bent on overturning superficial and exploitative power structures. The last time the world saw a Pluto-in-Scorpio generation was between the years of 1735 and 1747. This was a radical period of redefinition and realignment of power for societies all over the world. Most notably to Western historians, the American Revolution was fought largely by people born in the Pluto-in-Scorpio generation. These power-players come into the world ready to ask the hard questions and root out festering injustices. Pluto does not play.

If we don't work with Pluto's energy in our lives, or if we shy away from the hard lessons that this planet has to teach us, we can get stuck in the dark places that we are meant to learn from and pass through. Pluto's presence in the houses of your natal chart can indicate where there is a tendency for you to become obsessed, or where you're likely to encounter struggles for power. Plutonian energy can be possessive or manipulative if left unchecked. This is a manifestation of an energetic block and pushes us to ask ourselves: What are we holding on to that is keeping us from our power? When Pluto goes retrograde, this influence will be especially strong. We will be asked to make a choice about whether we will remain

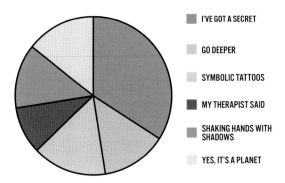

I'VE GOT A SECRET

GO DEEPER

SYMBOLIC TATTOOS

MY THERAPIST SAID

SHAKING HANDS WITH SHADOWS

YES, IT'S A PLANET

in relationships that have become codependent or smothering. Alternatively, if you're the one leading with fear or power-hungry tendencies, Pluto in retrograde will ensure that you loosen your grip—whether you want to or not. Pluto insists that we let go of the illusions of safety and jump into the unknown. Once we take that leap, we will be able to fully embrace Pluto's wisdom. What would it feel like for you to let go of what disturbs you? What would it feel like to relax into the uncertainty of life and to open yourself to transformation?

GLYPHS

Those little pictograph squiggles that show up in your birth chart? Those are glyphs, and they're not just cute symbols; they're derived from old symbols used in astrological notation. Astrologers use them to represent the placement of the planets in your birth chart. They've changed over the years, but the earliest version of the glyphs we use today date back to Europe in the Middle Ages. Today, they're mostly used as a kind of shorthand instead of a sign or planet's name written out entirely.

CAREER &
PUBLIC IMAGE

FRIENDSHIPS &
BELONGING

SPIRITUALITY &
THE SUBCONSCIOUS

SELF &
IDENTITY

MONEY &
VALUE

COMMUNICATION
& COMMUNITY

BELIEFS, LEARNING, & TRAVEL

SHARE RESOURCES & INTIMACY

COMMITTED PARTNERSHIPS

DAILY ROUTINES & HEALTH

CREATIVITY & ROMANTIC ENERGY

HOME & FAMILY

8

7

6

5

Navigating
the
Stars

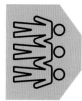

BRINGING IT HOME

With an understanding of the planets under our belts, we now embark on a crash course on the twelve houses, which are the key to unlocking what makes your birth chart so unique. The planets in your chart are each assigned a sign based on where they were in the sky when you took your very first breath. But astrologers have another trick up their sleeves to decode the cosmos—it's *where* the planets and signs live in your specific chart that makes it totally personalized.

Where the planets and signs represent inherent aspects of who we are—how we love, how we think, how we communicate—the houses are each associated with the different areas of our lives where we apply these basic energies.

Working with astrological houses isn't too tricky once you get a hang of it, but to help you along if you've never heard of these before, please accept our humble gift of yet another elaborate metaphor. One way to think about the houses that make up the interior of your chart is to imagine them as a friendly, weirdly circular neighborhood! And, just like any other cookie-cutter suburb in outer space, we all have the same houses in the same places, in charge of the same things—the first house is always in charge of the way we present ourselves to the world, and the fourth house is always in charge of family stuff, no matter whose chart we're looking at.

However, the denizens of your chart in this unnecessarily elaborate metaphor (the signs and planets) are nested into a given house the moment you're born, and it's different for each of us. Libra might live in the first house on your chart, but on your friend's chart, Pisces lives in the first house. This means that you might present yourself to the world with the signature Libran gift of gab, while your friend might present like a dreamy, sensitive Pisces because you have different

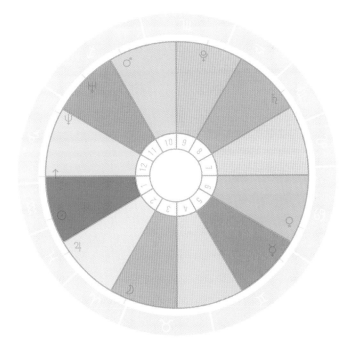

signs living in your first houses. TL;DR—the houses and their respective jobs stay the same, but the signs and planets that live there change from person to person, and so change how that part of your life is expressed.

Not only do the twelve houses correspond to the twelve areas of our lives, but they also each have an astrological sign that matches their energy as a default. These corresponding signs are called the natural rulers of a given house and they

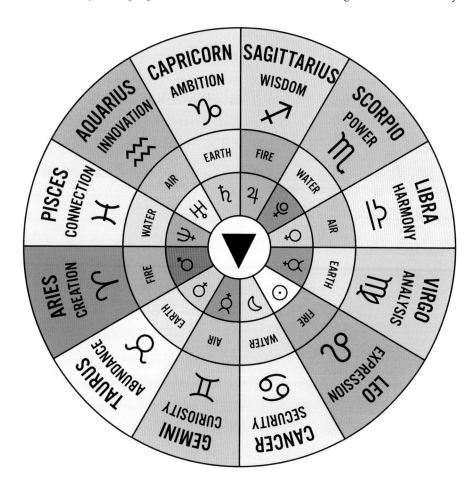

can help clarify what each house is about. For example, the first house is ruled by Aries, a sign of initiation and momentum, which makes sense, right? The natural rulers of each house are helpful to know because if you already know the basic qualities of an Aries and you learn that Aries is the natural ruler of the first house, then you're already clued in to that house's basic vibe.

They're not trying to get the answers to your security questions or steal your identity—they need this data to find out which sign was in your first house when you were born, a.k.a. what your rising sign is, in order to chart the rest of the houses.

You know that as much as we love memes and metaphors, we also love nuanced historical digressions! Just kidding (kind of). Now that you're clued in to what houses are, how they correspond to our lives and the different signs, and why the first house matters, we can dive into the details of which house rules what aspect of your life. But before we do, you just need a little background and which house system we use (this is the historical digression part).

We use the Placidus house system to create and interpret your chart. This system, named after an Italian monk and mathematician who was alive during the Renaissance and got credit for inventing this system (he didn't, but that's a long story), is the most popular system in contemporary astrology. There are other systems out there, like the whole sign system or the equal house system, but you don't need to worry about those. All you need to know is that the Placidus house

HOUSES

The houses in astrology are the twelve divisions of your chart that correspond to twelve different parts of your life, like your career, your love life, etc. The houses are the areas where we apply the different energies of the planets and signs.

system uses the sun's path through the sky to divide up the houses, and most of the time when people are talking about houses in astrology, they will be referring to this house system unless they specify otherwise. We could go on about the scintillating life and times of the Italian monk/mathematician who did not, in fact, create the system named after him if you want? No? Okay, fine, let's move on to the houses.

PLACIDUS

This is a system for dividing up the houses in astrology based on the sun's apparent journey through the sky over time. This system of house division takes its name from Italian monk and mathematician Placidus de Titis who used, but did not invent, the system. This is the most popular house system in Western contemporary astrology and also the system that we use at Sanctuary.

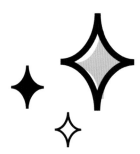

FIRST HOUSE

We've been hyping up this house—and for good reason! This is where it all begins for the houses, and for you! It rules your self-image, the first impressions you make, and how you respond to the world around you. Whichever signs or planets are present here become the energies that you wear on your sleeve. This house also shapes your appearance, and the way others perceive you. It corresponds with Aries energy, the fiery start of the zodiac. The signs or planets that occupy this house will have a strong influence on your life. For example, if the sun was in your first house, you may shine with that particular it-factor that makes a performer.

SECOND HOUSE

The second house is all about wealth and value. This house asks you to consider: what belongs to you, and how do you relate to ownership? It reveals what you value and how you express that. It makes sense that this house corresponds with Taurus, the resourceful bull. The signs and planets in your second house reveal a lot about how you accumulate resources in your life. For example, say you have lucky Jupiter and chatty Mercury in your second house— it might indicate fortunate opportunities come to you through networking.

THIRD HOUSE

The third house is all about communication. This includes the way you speak, write, and express yourself. It also rules networking, early education, and short trips. Ruled by Gemini, a sign given to spontaneous connections, this house is all about how you translate your inner world to the world at large. The signs and planets that appear in this house influence attitudes about communication. For example, if you have many planets energizing this house, you might find that you're inclined toward careers like writing or public speaking. Aquarius in this house may reveal a desire to lead a movement that makes a change in the world.

FOURTH HOUSE

Your fourth house deals with ideas of home, meaning your literal home as well as the feeling of home. What is private and intimate for you? Where and how do you feel most nurtured and safe? This house is also associated with family and, specifically, the mother archetype. Ruled by nurturing Cancer, the planets and signs that fall in your fourth house reveal the way that you relate to the most basic ideas of comfort, closeness, and the kind of intimacy you share with those you're closest to. Say you have Uranus in your fourth house—this may indicate that you're inclined toward unconventional living arrangements and family structures.

FIFTH HOUSE

The fifth house is the home of all things related to creativity, playfulness, and true love. This one is exciting, right? And, of course, it's ruled by luminous Leo, the big-hearted lion. The planets or signs that fall in this house reveal what we find entertaining and what gives us pleasure. If you have many planets lighting up your fifth house, you would likely be full of affection, creativity, and playfulness. If you have disciplined Saturn in your fifth house, you may find it difficult to cut loose and create freely.

SIXTH HOUSE

The sixth house gets physical. This is where your health, your work, and your desire to serve others all happily cohabitate. These areas of your life might seem different from each other at first, but when you consider that the natural ruler of this house is Virgo—the sign that loves consistent, effective action and is devoted to helping others—it starts to make sense. It's all tied to what you find useful in the physical realm. This house is associated with routines and the details of our lives. Say you have a whole squad of planets hanging out in the sixth house. In that case, you would be inclined to be a bit high-strung, but in a helpful way.

SEVENTH HOUSE

The seventh house is where relationships and marriage reside. Libra is the natural ruler of this house, and the scales are well-suited to represent the delicate balancing act of having a romantic partner in life. When you think of this house, think of words like "soul mate," "marriage," and "ideal partner." It is in this house that the planets and signs reveal what you need in romance, what kind of partnerships you'll likely have in life, and also how you relate to people who you don't like. Have Pisces in your seventh house? You might find yourself caught up in the fantasy of your ideal partner, instead of the reality of who they are.

EIGHTH HOUSE

Commonly known as the house of death, sex, and rebirth, this house can seem a little intimidating at first. But this house is the place where transformation happens—deep, first-hand experiences that fundamentally change who you are or how you think of yourself. Ruled by mysterious Scorpio, if your eighth house is full of planets, there's a good chance you'll spend your life feeling called to be close to the deep stuff. Think healing, hospice, midwifery, and therapists—vocations that deal with the most challenging aspects of our lives. With Venus in this house, you may find extraordinary beauty in the shadowy side of life.

NINTH HOUSE

The ninth house shows you where you are willing to push beyond the boundaries to seek out meaning in your life. It is often referred to as the house of long journeys because it is in this house that you learn how far you will go, physically and spiritually, to discover your life's purpose. It's no wonder that adventurous Sagittarius is the ruler of this house! When your ninth house has a lot of occupants, you might feel driven to see the world or to pursue an academic or philosophical life path. For example, if Aries falls in your ninth house, you likely have the spirit of an intrepid explorer who is always ready to jump into adventure.

TENTH HOUSE

The tenth house rules success and glory in your career and society. This house not only reveals career paths you should consider, but also tells you about how you relate to discipline and tradition. This sign is all about social status, ambition, and what material rewards mean to you. Capricorn, of course, is the natural ruler of this house. With a busy tenth house, you may have deep-seated ambition toward achieving a certain level of wealth and recognition. For example, if you have Gemini in your tenth house, this signals that the best path might be through some form of communication, like writing, teaching, or public speaking.

ELEVENTH HOUSE

The eleventh house shows your gifts and your visions for the future, of both community and friendship. It can tell us a lot about the kind of connections that impact your life. Ruled by Aquarius, this house is where you're called to the highest version of yourself. If you have a lot of planets in the eleventh house, this can indicate a powerful desire to serve the people around you in a way that brings people together, such as community organizing or campaigning. If, for example, you have Cancer in your eleventh house, you can expect to have many friends who are nurturing and protective of those they care about.

TWELFTH HOUSE

The twelfth house is interpreted in a few different ways. This is the house of spirituality, intuition, and potentialities that are yet to be fulfilled. With many planets in this placement, you might feel powerfully compelled by your subconscious desires, wounds, and drives. It makes sense that liminal Pisces rules this house, bringing all the psychic energy and deep compassion to the table. The denizens here reveal which aspects of yourself must be developed in order to transcend. For example, if you have Virgo in your twelfth house, you may find that you are overly self-sacrificing, putting others' needs before your own.

WHAT IF NO ONE'S HOME? UNDERSTANDING EMPTY HOUSES

You've seen your birth chart; you've been schooled in the meanings of planets, and how they live in your houses; and you're ready to set off on your journey to astrological mastery—but wait!

Although it can be disappointing when you don't have any planets or signs to analyze in a given area of your life, it's actually something you should welcome. Empty houses are traditionally understood as areas in your life that do not require too much attention. Traditionally, an empty house is related to the idea that you've already worked out the major kinks in that arena during a past life. But you don't have to believe in past lives for empty houses to make sense.

When you have a planet or a group of planets in one house, it means that it's an area of your life that draws a lot of your attention. Each planetary placement brings gifts as well as challenges. Imagine that you had disciplinarian Saturn, hot-headed Mars, and eccentric Uranus in your tenth house of career and glory. That lineup of planets would require a lot of attention to channel all that intense energy in productive ways. But say your tenth house was empty. This wouldn't mean that you would have no career! Instead, it means that work is not the center of your life or one of your main motivators. See? Empty houses are nothing to fear.

TRANSITS

Your birth chart is static, but the stars are always on the move. When they run their races around the solar system, they enter and exit the different signs at different times, sometimes hanging out together or far apart. (Sometimes they even seem to slide backward.) Their movements are called "transits." Learning about transits may sound less juicy than reading about the impact of your rising sign or your moon sign, we get it. It's not *you*, exactly. However, the transits are constantly impacting you, and understanding astrological transits is vitally important to get a sense of how astrologers write spooky-accurate horoscopes day-to-day or month-to-month.

As we mentioned, a transit is when a planet moves (which, IDK if you've heard, but that's, like, their favorite thing to do). The interesting thing about all that planetary movement is that each time one of those bad boys is in transit, it shifts the energy of the cosmos in subtle and not so subtle ways, depending on a bunch of different factors like which planet is in transit, how that transit interacts with your birth chart and other planets, and how long of an orbit a planet has.

Interpreting the effects of these transits is the main way that astrologers write your daily or monthly horoscopes.

When you open your favorite app to read your horoscope for that day, do you ever wonder how the astrologer knows all that information about how you might be feeling or what might stand out to you about the day? Well, it's not exactly magic, but it is a little bit complicated.

The first time you read a horoscope, it was probably a free horoscope for your sun sign, right? That's the way most of us start. It makes a lot of sense, because the sun sign is the most accessible bit of astrological information. All you need to know is the date you were born, not the time and place—easy-breezy, now you know astrology, right? Eh, not quite.

To get a full picture of what exactly you're looking at when you read a horoscope, daily or otherwise, you need to know the basics of what a horoscope actually is and how astrologers write them—this is where transits come in.

A horoscope is a kind of planetary weather report. Astrologers look at planetary transits happening that day or week or month and interpret how the transits they observe will impact a whole group of people who share the same sun sign. We all share the same sky, which means that we all have the same transits to work

TRANSITS

The planets are constantly in motion. When a planet passes through a sign or a position in a horoscope, we call that movement a "transit." The transits of the inner planets have less pronounced impacts because they move relatively quickly through the zodiac. The slower-moving planets have more impactful transits, are more powerful, and their effects are more noticeable.

with. But because the planets are in different placements in everyone's charts, the same transit will impact each person, even within the same sun sign, differently.

When astrologers write a daily horoscope, they are often observing the transit of the moon, not the sun. Tracking the moon is the best way to write a daily horoscope because the moon changes signs every two or two-and-a-half days, and each transit of the moon impacts our emotions and our inner world. So how does this become a daily horoscope . . . that you end up reading . . . for your sun sign? Excellent question! It can get technical here, but basically, an astrologer puts your sun sign in the first house and then the rest of the houses in order of the zodiac. For example, let's say your sun is in Capricorn on your birth chart and that the moon is in Virgo today. To write your horoscope today, an astrologer would put Capricorn in the first house and then look at which house in your chart is ruled by Virgo. It's okay if you're sweating this bit, but the basic idea is: where the moon goes, so does your mood. That's not such a surprise if you know about your moon sign!

Luckily, you don't have to track the transits of the moon and calculate angles and all that to read your daily horoscope. It's just important to know *how* these horoscopes are written so you can get a sense of the context. As a bonus, now that you know how astrologers write a horoscope, you'll know why it's so important to read the horoscope for your rising sign as well as your sun sign. It makes sense for astrologers to write horoscopes by putting sun signs in the first house because the sun is the chart's luminary, and this method gives you a big picture of your life. But you should also read a horoscope for your rising sign, because when astrologers write a daily horoscope, they put whatever sign they are writing for into the first house, remember? That means that a daily horoscope for your rising sign gives you equally important information about the area of your life that your first house rules.

See what we mean about transits being way juicier than they might seem on the surface? Learning about the astrological significance of transits is the key to understanding how all the different bits of astrological information fit together and impact you. This extra information will help you understand how your birth chart connects to the current movements of the planets, especially the moon when we're talking about the creation of your daily horoscope.

The moon deserves some special attention. The moon is not only one of the celestial bodies that influences our lives, but it also represents the emotional center of your psyche and constantly moves in a way that has meaning for us. Just like our emotions are ephemeral and always shifting, the moon has phases that also shape our inner world. Buckle your spacesuits, friends—it's time to go to the moon!

PS: Do you think spacesuits have buckles or, like, Velcro? Maybe magnets? Get back to us.

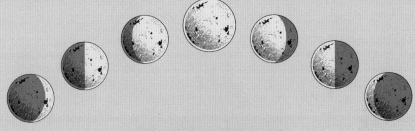

MOON CYCLES

The moon doesn't always get its fair share of attention in popular astrology! Sure, we talk about your moon sign (a.k.a. your natal moon), but people don't pay as much attention to the moon cycles. The moon goes through eight cycles every twenty-nine(ish) days. The moon's cycles today and the cycle you were born under both exert an influence on our lives. Think of each full cycle of the moon's phases mirroring the full cycle of plant growth from seed to flower—whatever is planted at the beginning of the cycle matures over the course of the cycle and blooms at the full moon. We'll tell you a little about how the moon's energy shifts during each phase of the moon cycle, and how the phase of your natal moon might play into the whole lunar dynamic.

NEW MOON

If the new moon were described by an agricultural metaphor, this would be the part of the metaphor where you would be a farmer, rising before dawn to look out on your freshly turned fields. The sky is dark, but the sun is on the horizon. What are you going to plant this month? The new moon is the perfect time to make plans and set goals. In the quiet dark of a new moon, you have the space to step back, take a breath, and reassess. People born under the new moon tend to lead with their intuition and feel inspired by fresh starts.

WAXING CRESCENT

During the waxing crescent phase of the moon cycle, we are spurred into action. This is the time to start digging the holes and planting the seeds. You gather your tools and sweep the floors. You begin to feel your gaze focusing on what drives you and what you want out of it. Where the new moon was that first burst of creation, the waxing crescent is when you start settling in to the work. As this is a moment in the lunar cycle where your determination is at an all-time high, if you were born beneath a waxing crescent, you tend toward internal motivation, a strong sense of purpose, and a determined nature.

FIRST QUARTER

In the moon's first quarter, we feel empowered to make decisions and take action. At this stage, the moon looks half full. This is the time for you to collect all your courage and start taking bigger steps, putting yourself out there, and taking risks. This is a period you may be asked to demonstrate your commitment to the intentions you set at the beginning of the cycle. As a natal lunar phase, this moon indicates that regardless of the moon's sign, the individual will possess an inner fortitude that treats all obstacles as a minor inconvenience. This is the phase of perseverance and the drive to cross the finish line.

WAXING GIBBOUS

The moon looks almost full at this stage, and the energy is a heady blend of passion from the nearness of the full moon mixed in with the impulse to reassess your options. Although there is tons of momentum during this period, learning to work with a waxing gibbous strategically means being able to take a step back from the forward motion and think about how to respond to the circumstances of the moment with intention. Those with a waxing gibbous as their natal moon phase tend to be accumulators, collectors of all kinds. This natal phase signals a basic drive to improve and expand.

FULL MOON

It's here! The full moon lights up the night and puts a confident spring in your step. This is the lunar effect at its brightest and most pronounced. You become acutely aware of the effect, good or bad, that you have on others. In the light of the full moon, anything that was hidden will come to light. If you were born in the light of a full moon, you tend to be firmly grounded in your beliefs: externally stubborn and controversial, while internally constantly pulled in different directions by the struggle between their emotions versus their calculating, logical mind.

WANING GIBBOUS

The waning gibbous phase, also called the disseminating moon phase, asks us to refine our plans and our intentions. Whatever has come to light during the full moon must be responded to in kind during the waning gibbous moon. If any loose ends have come to your attention, now is the time to take those threads and decide whether you'll toss them or make something new. As a natal phase, the waning gibbous shapes people who are not afraid to put up a fight if the cause is just. These are people who feel driven to prove themselves to the world and become devoted to causes that move them.

THIRD QUARTER

As the moon begins to shed its light and thin its crescent, you might feel a burden being lifted. This is a time where you'll find that letting go of what is not authentic to who you are will be easier. All of the growth and refinement of the previous phases work to accumulate energy and guide that energy in a particular direction. This is the time to let the necessary things fall away. If the moon was in its third-quarter phase when you were born, you were not born to be a follower. With natal third-quarter moon, you are undeterred by conflict and dedicated to the greater good.

WANING CRESCENT

The waning crescent shows us the last of the moon's light and asks us to set down our burdens and take a load off. Rest and stillness are necessary parts of the process of growth, and during the waning crescent, you shouldn't feel bad about taking some time for yourself. You'll need this regeneration stage to fortify you for the burst of new energy on the horizon at the start of the next cycle. As a natal moon phase, the waning crescent represents a connection to higher powers and a strong sense of destiny. Those born under this moon tend to turn their gaze upward, always seeking guidance from the forces greater than themselves.

YOUR NATAL MOON

Like everything else in astrology, the moon cycle does not exist in a vacuum and the energy associated with each phase does not touch all of our lives in the same way. As the moon cycles through its phases, the subtle influence of the lunar shifts affects our internal, emotional experience, and this impact is felt differently depending on your natal moon. When you were born, your emotional center was formed by the parameters of the sign the moon was in, the moon's aspects, and the lunar phase.

If your moon sign is the whole landscape of your inner world, then you could think of the phase of your natal moon as the climate of that landscape. Like the weather pattern of a particular region, our natal moon phase indicates the basic vibration that our feelings and beliefs tend to take. Just because it's always sunny in LA doesn't mean that there isn't the occasional storm, but storms don't change the overall sunshiny vibe.

Working with your natal moon phase is a way to pay close attention to the connection between the tides of your inner ocean and the pull of the ancient moon. Today's moon phase might amplify, minimize, harmonize, or conflict with your natal moon phase. Tracking the lunar cycle allows us to rest in the knowledge that change is the only constant in this universe and that no matter how things feel right now, you can count on a new perspective offered up by whatever the moon has in store for us next.

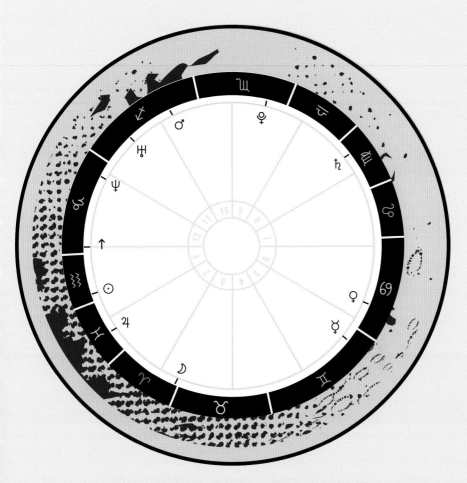

*Your moon sign is a key part of how you use astrology in your daily life,
and plays a huge role in your horoscope, too.*

PLANETARY PROGRESS

You remember science class. The planets of our solar system are always moving, rotating, whirling through space. If you think about the signs like a wheel around the planet Earth, as the planets move through the sky from your vantage point on Earth, those movers and shakers travel in and out of the "zones" of specific signs. A planetary ingress in astrology simply means that a planet has moved from within one sign to another. That simple definition is all you need to know to get a basic sense of different events that astrologers are describing when they talk about Mercury entering Pisces or Venus entering Aries. But if you were the kind of kid who never got tired of every parent's favorite never-ending game, of "But, why?" and you haven't grown out of it, then welcome. We love asking "why." So why *do* planets change signs?

As you know, planets are always moving in their orbits, and astrologers are always tracking the path of those planets as they traverse the zodiac day after day, month after month, and year after year. Each planet has a different timing for its ingress because each planet is moving at a different speed relative to the other planets. You already know that the moon ingresses every two-and-a-half days and that astrologers use this movement to write our daily horoscopes. This isn't because there's a grand conspiracy by a moon cult to take over the world of astrology, nor is it because the moon is the most important and meaningful celestial body. The other planets all have ingresses that make them either too fast for their impacts to be noticeably felt, like Mercury or Mars, or too slow to be felt on a day-to-day basis, like Saturn or Jupiter. You might still feel big moments in those planets' movements, especially when they tangle together, but the moon is ol' reliable in terms of impacting your day-to-day life. If it's powerful enough to pull the tides, it's not surprising that it might tug on your heartstrings, too.

But why does the speed of a planetary ingress matter? Well, you might be catching on to the fact that astrology takes on almost every concept from the big broad strokes all the way down to the minute details. Planetary ingresses are a great example of this because they operate on a large scale but have incremental transformations all the time. When a planet ingresses into a new sign—say, when Venus enters Aries—this is a noticeable shift of Venus's tone. Venus, the ruler of love and beauty, moves into Aries and is suddenly illuminated with spontaneous and direct bravado. That is the big tone shift. The smaller, incremental shift is what happens to Venus's tone while in Aries's fiery sign. At the start of the process, our romantic mood is beginning to open up to all the possibilities that confident and seductive Aries brings to the table. This influence builds throughout the ingress, developing, blooming, and intensifying. The longer a planet takes to move into another sign, the longer and more impactful that particular planetary motion will be on our lives.

To work with planetary sign changes, you want to consider a few different factors. Although we all share the same sky, watch the same planets in their orbits, and get a sense of each movement's general theme, the impacts are felt differently for each of us because each of us has different natal charts. . . . don't you think that sentence would be great on a t-shirt? Okay, maybe not. But it is a super important thing to remember when learning about the world of astrology. Going back to our Venus in Aries ingress example for a moment, let's say that your natal

Venus is also in Aries. This would mean that your basic attitude toward all things love and beauty is assertive, honest, and passionate.

When a planet aligns with the position that it was in when you were born, it takes the foundational energy of that planet in your life and amplifies it, brings an issue full circle, and/or draws your attention strongly to that area of your life. If this is too deep in the weeds for you but you still want to know how to approach your next grand seduction, you can always hit up an astrologer. Working with an astrologer is fun not only because they are generally nice people with an affinity for herbal tea, heartfelt convos, and big moods, etc., but also because these hyper-detailed nuances that might turn off normal people are *precisely* their jam.

INGRESS

As you know, planets move around the sun and so are always on the move in the sky. When a planet moves into a new sign or a new house, that is a planetary ingress. It literally means to enter or go into. An ingress signals a change in the tone or personality of the given planet.

RETROGRADES

At this point, you're an expert in planetary movement, so we thought we'd throw a curveball your way—it's time to talk retrogrades. As astrologers watch the skies, sometimes they'll spot a planet that seems to be moving in reverse and generally bouncing around in the sky.

Of course, the laws of physics still apply and planets don't reverse their motion—it just looks that way because of the movement of our Earth relative to whichever planet is out there looking all topsy-turvy. This weird phenomenon has gotten a lot of press in popular astrology with the help of the bad behavior of Mercury retrograde, which more and more people are talking about as it enters the mainstream. If you haven't heard, the general understanding of Mercury retrograde is that it's a time when plans go awry, when you lose your keys or accidentally send a text meant for your best friend to your boss instead. And, okay, we have to admit that all of these regular human faux pas might be more common in times where Mercury, ruler of communication, goes off its path, but that's not the whole story.

During Venus, Mercury, and Mars retrograde, these planets are active and have a huge impact on your life, but not in the usual ways. The areas of your psyche that they influence refuse to be ignored during retrograde and they pack a lot of energy. These planets move farther off their track during retrogrades than the planets that are farther out there in the celestial neighborhood, which results in more exaggerated and eccentric behavior. These retrogrades, which penetrate to the very heart of our psychic core, feel personal, challenging, and ask more of us than lucky Jupiter or stately Saturn do during their retrogrades. These guys are in retrograde, like, one-third of the time and their deviations from their normal path are less extreme. This means that their impacts feel less personal and less generally challenging.

When a planet strays from its normally neat path along its elliptic course, it disrupts its usual behavior and in turn disrupts whatever behaviors are "usual" for us. Astrology is not all rainbows and affirmations all the time, just as life is not like that all the time. During the times that a planet has disruptions in their business as usual, we might think of this as the planet wandering off the beaten path and exploring other possibilities. Retrogrades are a time to slow down, to reflect on the choices you make in the area of life that the retrograding planet impacts, and to have compassion for wherever you're at in your journey. As the planets spin, they reveal all sort of choices and paths for us to follow. The choice of where to go is up to you!

RETROGRADE

When a planet appears to be moving in reverse in the sky, we call that a retrograde. Here, the operative word is "appears." Planets do not *actually* move backward—it is an optical illusion that appears to us because of our vantage point on the Earth. This phenomenon occurs in the same way that a car in the next lane might look like it is moving backward as you drive past it.

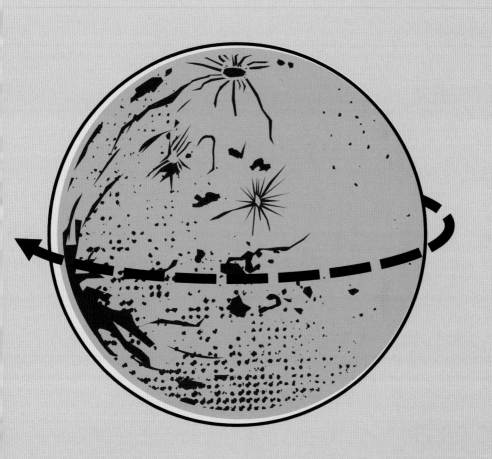

ARIES	Bold, Passionate, Excited	♈
TAURUS	Grounded, Generous, Dependable	♉
GEMINI	Curious, Clever, Chatty	♊
CANCER	Intuitive, Protective, Nurturing	♋
LEO	Dramatic, Warm, Proud	♌
VIRGO	Loyal, Organized, Devoted	♍
LIBRA	Graceful, Fair, Charming	♎
SCORPIO	Magnetic, Intense, Powerful	♏
SAGITTARIUS	Adventurous, Hopeful, Wise	♐
CAPRICORN	Ambitious, Caring, Helpful	♑
AQUARIUS	Thoughtful, Inventive, Fascinated	♒
PISCES	Dreamy, Empathetic, Creative	♓

SUN	Act, Perform, Be	☉
MOON	Process, Feel, Reflect	☽
MERCURY	Express, Connect, Communicate	☿
VENUS	Love, Value, Celebrate	♀
MARS	Decide, Fight, Achieve	♂
JUPITER	Expand, Indulge, Grow	♃
SATURN	Build, Analyze, Control	♄
URANUS	Rebel, Create, Innovate	♅
NEPTUNE	Dream, Imagine, Transcend	♆
PLUTO	Transform, Empower, Remember	♇

The
Signs

SNACKING	SUDDEN INSPIRATION	HOT SHOWER	PETTY COMPETITIONS	INDOOR AEROBICS
YELLING	NEW PROJECT	PUMP UP PLAYLIST	ICED COFFEE	PARKOUR
ARGUMENTS	RUNNING LATE	*Free*	I'M RIGHT!	TEMPER TANTRUM
SMALL FIRES	WINNING	APOLOGIZING	345 TEXTS UNREAD	SCREAM THERAPY
RUNNING	ATHLEISURE	PACING	NEW HOBBY	VOICE MEMOS

Aries

DATES	ELEMENT	MODALITY
March 21–April 20	Fire	Cardinal

Who has the time to wait for some outside force to define your personality? Certainly not you, Aries. You're the self-assured leader of the zodiac, charging into the fray headfirst as the first sign of the astrological year. Your sign is represented by the ram and ruled by fiery Mars, the god of war who bestows the gifts of audacity, confidence, and decisiveness, and is fundamentally passionate and fearless. Although you may have moments of doubt, at your core, you have an unshakeable sense of purpose. Your power comes from your ability to initiate action and galvanize others.

Like the ram, you're a steadfast cardinal sign that heralds not only the first days of spring, but as the first sign in the zodiac, you are the astrological leader of the pack. Your fiery nature takes the nebulous revelations of the Pisces season and turns them into ambition, action, and a rallying cry to those around you. You're a

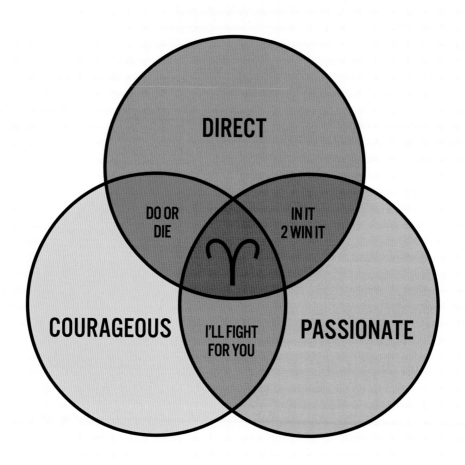

motivator, capable of sweeping others up into your drive and enthusiasm. Where others would lose sight of the higher vision, your eyes shine with ambition.

The fearlessness you are known for comes, in part, from the fact that you are the youngest sign of the zodiac. You emerge from an astrological blank slate, bringing new ideas and contagious enthusiasm into the world. Each sign learns from its predecessor, but with no inherited wisdom to learn from the signs that came before you, you must make your own way in the world. Don't worry, Aries, there's no one better suited for this unique path. Where others would see an insurmountable challenge, you see an opportunity to forge your own path. Look before you leap? Forget it—you've already vaulted across in the time it takes for others to formulate a plan.

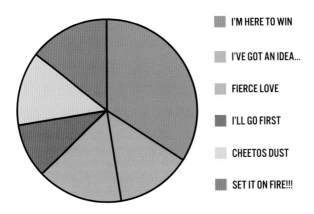

I'M HERE TO WIN

I'VE GOT AN IDEA...

FIERCE LOVE

I'LL GO FIRST

CHEETOS DUST

SET IT ON FIRE!!!

You move through the world looking straight ahead, single-mindedly charging toward your goals, easily drawing others to your cause. You can't help it. People are drawn to your straightforward manner; they believe in you, and they trust you to make a firm decision and stand by it. You'll always require new mountains to climb and new worlds to discover. What's the fun in reaching the top if it means the journey is over? It's in your nature to act first and think later. With your bravery and determination, you're prepared to push through whatever obstacles this charge-ahead approach might generate in your path through life.

RELATIONSHIPS

It's no surprise that your signature passion and assertive nature carry over into your relationships. You tend to be a more dominant partner, but this doesn't necessarily mean you're a control freak! It's just that one of your gifts is a clear sense of yourself. You know what you want and need—as far as you're concerned, it is an expression of love to tell your partner exactly what's on your mind. As you learn and grow into your most authentic self, you'll be able to loosen up and pick your battles more carefully. This means, occasionally, letting your partner chart the course.

Speaking of partners, you need someone who can keep up. Your enthusiasm and confidence are your special brand of charm. Your uncomplicated nature is a breath of fresh air in a massively complex world. You like things to move fast, and there's nothing wrong with that! You just need to choose partners that are equally ready to dive in. However, if you find that you're trying to fit someone else into your ideas about who they should be, you might want to step back. Sometimes you have to zoom out for the high-level view to appreciate what you have. Without a big-picture perspective, you could miss the forest for the trees. Don't try to change your partner with criticism and ultimatums. Instead, do your best to live by your values and inspire others by the example you set. Seek out friends and partners that embody qualities of Libra, your astrological opposite. Libra's tact and careful nature will temper your quick reflexes and balance your fire. The goal here is not to change who you are but to soften your edges and expand your horizon.

- ANGRY
- CONFIDENT
- COURAGEOUS
- STILL ANGRY
- EXCITED

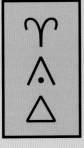

LIKES	DISLIKES
A firm yes	Being told no
Paralleled excitement	Commitment
Making a statement	Not standing out

SKILLS	STRUGGLES
Giving their opinion	Not giving their opinions
Taking the lead	Being a team player
Brainstorming	Following through

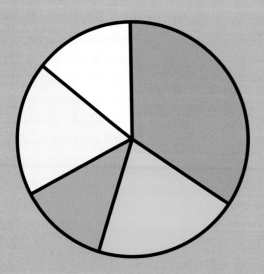

- ■ SELF-STARTING
- ■ CONFIDENT
- ■ CREATIVE
- ■ ENERGETIC
- ■ FRESH

CAREER

You would rather make things happen now than get bogged down with all the details. You'll always be the one to get projects off the ground, to light a fire under your colleagues, and push the boundaries of your field. The path to the top for you lies in whatever challenges you the most. Like the ram, you navigate daunting terrain with a surefooted gait. You're ready to push aside obstacles. You don't worry about making a mistake, because every mistake pushes you forward and refines your abilities.

As the first sign in the zodiac, you have a taste for coming in at the top spot. You're ambitious, competitive, and motivated by new experiences. Any career that requires discovery and mastery will keep you engaged long-term. You'll want plenty of opportunities to roll your sleeves up and get your hands dirty. The catch? Your direct, no-nonsense personality might set you up to step on toes once in a while. Give others space to contribute; patience is key. Consider climbing career ladders that have clear rungs like athletics, politics, or work in finance—careers that depend on good instincts and a daring personality. No matter which path you choose, take time for rest and reflection. You may feel restless when you hit the pause button, but this time is never wasted. It's necessary for you to stay tuned in to your intuition so that you don't chase accolades just for the sake of adding another trophy to the shelf.

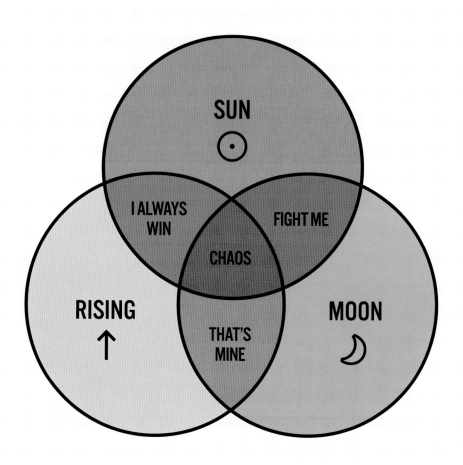

This is just the beginning, Aries! To take things a little deeper, read about what it means for Aries to be your sun, moon, or rising sign. Each placement shapes your personality in a few different ways.

ARIES SUN

The sun is the guiding light of your chart. It orients all the other qualities that make up your personality. This luminous energy in Aries supercharges the fiery, strong-willed energy native to the sign. You have a sharp mind, and one of your greatest strengths is your ability to see through distraction and clutter and stay focused on what is truly important to you. At times, you can be impatient, because the unpredictable nature of life can be a source of frustration for a go-getter like you. Balance and fulfillment lie in learning to compromise without sacrificing the integrity of your vision.

DRIVEN   SELFISH
ENTHUSIASTIC   IMPATIENT

ARIES MOON

The placement of the moon in your chart shapes your emotional landscape, and in your case, the landscape is a dramatic series of peaks and valleys. Aries has a reputation for hot-headedness, but the energy is not so deterministic. It may be first nature for you to take offense if you feel you've been disrespected or ignored. Try not to lash out, and look inward instead. Ask yourself what you need to feel safe and understood. If you're feeling disconnected or drained, spark your excitement by being more spontaneous and allowing life to surprise you.

INDEPENDENT DYNAMIC

COMPETITIVE REACTIONARY

ARIES RISING

As far as first impressions are concerned, it's hard to find a sign that makes their mark with as much flair as you do, Aries. You don't need any premeditated conversation starters—you are the conversation starter. Your straightforward nature can intimidate some but is a breath of fresh air to others. You are a relentless conversationalist and never run out of new ideas or new points to argue over. Five minutes of conversation with an Aries rising is all the time you'd need to come away with the knowledge that you are speaking to someone trustworthy, true, and definitely formidable.

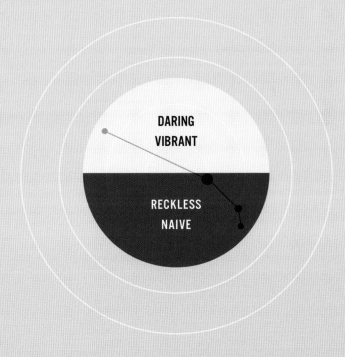

DARING
VIBRANT

RECKLESS
NAIVE

NAPTIME	MY WARDROBE	LOUNGEWEAR	NO THANKS	HUNGRY
#NATURE	REDECORATING	CUP OF TEA	IS THAT MARBLE?	GROWTH
NEW SKILLS	PANTRY GOALS	Free	PERIOD PIECES	INTERIOR DESIGN
AVOCADO TOAST	#LUXURIATING	GARDENING	LET'S STAY IN	FRESH FLOWERS
CUDDLEFEST	MORE CANDLES	TIME TO LEAVE	MORE CHEESE	FOUR-COURSE MEALS

Taurus

DATES	ELEMENT	MODALITY
April 20–May 20	Earth	Fixed

An expert in all things pleasurable, Taurus, your inner compass points you toward beauty and sensuality. Like your celestial representative the bull, you are a peaceful creature when you are in your own territory, surrounded by pleasant pastures. As an earth sign ruled by Venus, the planet of love, beauty, and money, you are firmly grounded in the material world while also having a preference for the very best it has to offer. In short? You've got a case of champagne tastes. Literally. Taureans are the gourmands of the zodiac, and no one loves an elaborate meal and bottomless glasses of fine wine like you do.

Unfortunately, caviar doesn't grow on trees. Your appetite for finer things is going to take cash. Lucky for you, the bull does not shy away from hard work. When you decide that you want something, you'll move heaven and earth to get it. In pursuit of your goals, you are ambitious, focused, and not easily deterred.

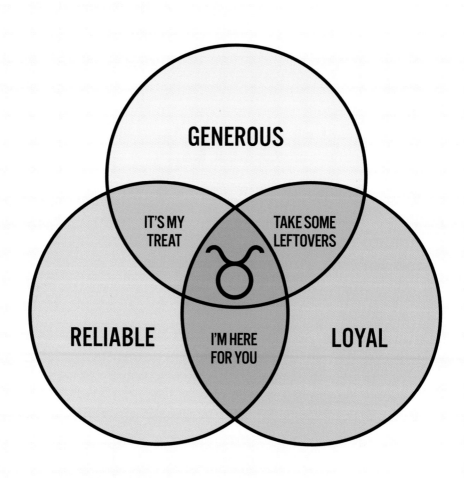

Taurus, you take all of Aries's quick-to-act impulsivity and bring it back down to earth. Aries's fire would burn bright and fast and die out without you steadily adding fuel to keep the flame alight. Taurus season is a time to feel deeply, emotionally, and physically, and to find your roots.

The determination and stability associated with Taurus are amplified by the fixed quality of your sign. You're always looking out to the horizon, setting your sights on the long game. You have the ability to filter out distractions and keep moving forward. The definition of integrity, you stand your ground. The challenge for you is to stay flexible when circumstances change.

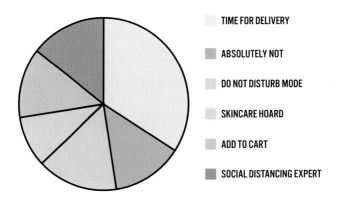

- TIME FOR DELIVERY
- ABSOLUTELY NOT
- DO NOT DISTURB MODE
- SKINCARE HOARD
- ADD TO CART
- SOCIAL DISTANCING EXPERT

In your quest for stability, you might find yourself bulldozing over other people's needs in decision-making. But when it comes to intimacy, you're *all about* making sure everyone gets their needs met. You are an excellent communicator and you love to make other people happy.

RELATIONSHIPS

Your love languages are reliability and sensuality. Unlike changeable air signs or impulsive fire signs, Taurus, what you see is what you get in terms of your emotional character. If you encountered a Taurus in the wild, you'd know it. At a bar, you might find a Taurus lingering near the bar discussing digestifs. At a party, a Taurus might be surrounded by admirers complimenting the always-elegant bull on their stylish look. If you have Taurus in your chart, especially if your Venus is in Taurus or it's your rising sign, you might be hard to get but great to keep.

A potential love interest would need to skip the small talk to turn your head. You value deep conversation and sustained interest. You might come off as stoic at first due to your tendency to move slowly. You love to be wined and dined. Even though you're the opposite of shallow, a shiny present with a big bow would go a long way to wooing you. Once you're smitten with a special someone, you are an incredibly loyal and affectionate partner. The people you love count on you to think of the little things that others would miss. Though you might be a bit stubborn sometimes, the right person will find that the depth of your love makes up for it.

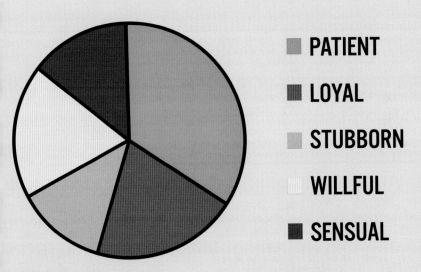

- ■ PATIENT
- ■ LOYAL
- ■ STUBBORN
- ■ WILLFUL
- ■ SENSUAL

LIKES	DISLIKES
2,000 thread count	Scratchy fabric
Calling the shots	Motels
Moisturized skin & hair	Bad hair days

SKILLS	STRUGGLES
Toughing it out	Admitting defeat
Being in charge	Delegating anything
Spotting opportunities	Changing their mind

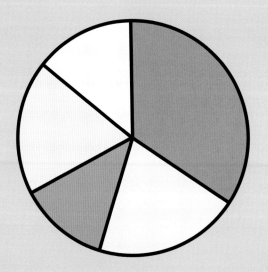

- CONSISTENT
- RELIABLE
- TACTFUL
- PLEASANT
- RESOURCEFUL

CAREER

In their career, Taurus will put one foot in front of the other until they get where they set out to go. As a fixed earth sign, Taurus really *gets* how to take a vision, break it into small steps, and execute each step methodically. If you commit yourself to something, you're in it for the long haul. Count on Taurus to do what they do for the right reasons, as the bull isn't breaking a sweat for clout and likes. They're all about results for results' sake.

Although you can be an excellent team player, Taurus, you have a reputation for being stubborn, and your straightforward demeanor can rub some people the wrong way. As much as Taurus loves to acquire luxurious pleasures, the bull also craves security. Taurus would do well in a career that gives them the latitude to take action and progress slowly and steadily toward their goals, or in creative pursuits that keep Taurus's body moving. The key to working with Taurus: don't get between the bull and what they're chasing.

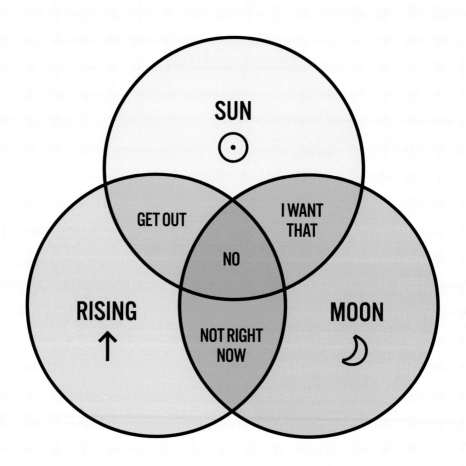

Taurus energy is fundamentally sensual and earthy; however, this manifests differently if your sun, moon, or rising sign is in the territory of the celestial bull. Each of these defines distinct elements of your personality, your emotional world, and the first impression you make.

TAURUS SUN

If your sun is in Taurus, the source of your sanity is a sensual experience. When you slip into a warm bubble bath, wrap yourself in a silky robe, or make an elaborate meal to enjoy with your lucky loved ones, you're not being self-indulgent—you're feeding your soul. You emanate grounded self-awareness. Your energy is like a magnet to those who lack your stable sense of self. This can lead to healing and profound relationships, but at times your commitment to seeing things through might blind you to the downsides of a situation. The best advice from the stars for a Taurus sun? Learn to let go a little bit. Your fixation on the material can lead you away from the true abundance in your life. Work toward generosity and you'll see your sense of well-being multiply.

GROUNDED RIGID
GENEROUS MATERIALISTIC

TAURUS MOON

A Taurus moon signals an emotional drive for comfort and security. Sensuous pleasures stir your soul. You're able to keep a cool head where others might lose their temper. You're able to slow down and feel your emotions in your body. You're an excellent listener, and you provide a safe harbor for other people's feelings. However, if you do a bit of journaling and self-reflection, you might find that you struggle with feeling emotionally stuck. You have to pick your battles. With your moon in Taurus, balance comes from practicing compassion and flexibility, even when you're sure you're right.

STABLE CLINGY

COMFORTABLE PETTY

TAURUS RISING

If your rising sign is Taurus, you attract others to you like moths to a flame. Let's just get one thing out of the way—people adore you. Maybe it's your stylish aesthetic, your steady energy, or the way you make others feel. You put people at ease and point them toward pleasure. You like for things to go according to plan, and sudden change is challenging for you. Practice spontaneity and vulnerability. It may feel like a trust-fall into the unknown, but you can trust that you'll have a crowd of people lining up to catch you.

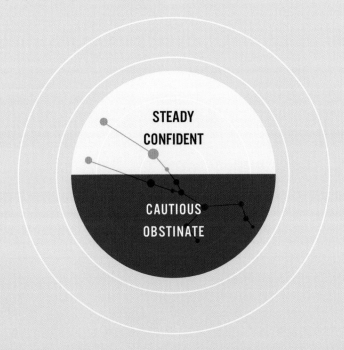

STEADY
CONFIDENT

CAUTIOUS
OBSTINATE

ANNOTATING	SPONTANEOUSLY	YES, AND?	GROUP TEXT	ZING!
THANK U NEXT	TWINNING	ACTUALLY	EASY BREEZY	EXPERIMENTS
MMORPGS	WHY IS THAT	Free	LIVE-TWEETING	MY LIBRARY CARD
MEET MY FRIENDS	LEARNING	BUZZING	PLAYING CARDS	ICED COFFEE
LOOSE WIRES	WHAT'S THAT?	DND MODE	TEDX MY HOUSE	JOT THAT DOWN

Gemini

DATES	ELEMENT	MODALITY
May 21–June 20	Air	Mutable

The trick to describing you, Gemini, is in not trying to pin you down. Your sign is represented by the twins and ruled by androgynous Mercury, the winged messenger god who can easily go from the heights of Olympus to the depths of Hades's underworld. You delight in your ability to shapeshift, to go wherever the wind takes you.

You're a mutable air sign, after all. The last sign of spring and the first air sign of the zodiac, you are the breath that takes those seeds planted in Taurus season and whisks them to the far corners of the earth, where they'll be watered and nurtured by Cancer season and the start of summer. But until then, these new ideas are yours to do with what you will. The question is: What will you do with them?

It's not like you'll have a short supply of interesting ways to apply your clever ideas. You're endlessly curious. Imaginative. Bored easily. On the internet, you

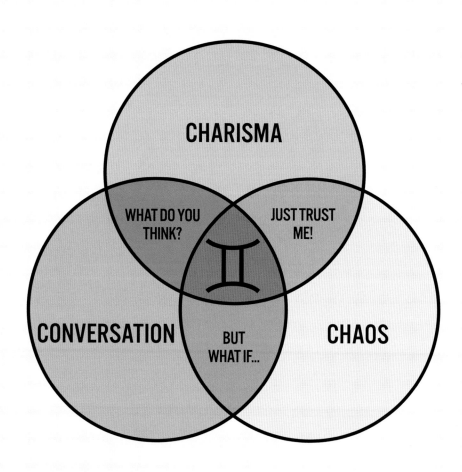

get a bad rap. But you know that. Here's the thing: certain narratives in our society just don't fit you. You are less interested in fitting in than you are in arriving at new synergies. You crave innovation. If you love what you do, you never work a day in your life. You don't have to work to find your passion. You are someone who absorbs all the ideas the world has to offer and delights in sharing them with everyone you meet along the way. You cross-pollinate inspiration as you move through the world.

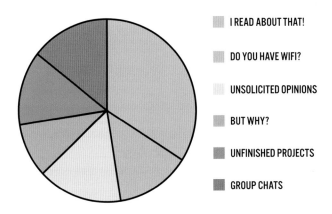

- I READ ABOUT THAT!
- DO YOU HAVE WIFI?
- UNSOLICITED OPINIONS
- BUT WHY?
- UNFINISHED PROJECTS
- GROUP CHATS

Communication and intellectual stimulation are vital; you absorb new ideas in pop culture, technology, and whatever fields interest you as easily as other people breathe. As the gifted communicator that you are, you will need to find constant outlets for all the inspiration bubbling up inside of you. Your curiosity is one of the most important things about you, and staying flexible is the key to happiness. Too much structure just ties you down.

RELATIONSHIPS

Some signs need a lot of freedom, but for you it's more that you need to be free to talk to (and maybe flirt with!) anyone at the party. People are just interesting to you in a profoundly fundamental way, and discovering that is how you recharge. This is particularly true for Gemini moons. That doesn't mean you can't commit, but you're likely to need your lover to accept your many friends, acquaintances, and busy socializing schedule without feeling left out.

The list of your traits that friends and lovers adore tends to run long. At the top of the list? Your quick wit and surprising mind. Those close to you never have to worry about being bored. You need a partner that values variety. You're more of a *let's try that new fusion spot with the floor pillows and hookahs* kind of person than you are a regular at the local dive. Compromise is a necessary part of any intimate relationship, and for you, this means slowing down and giving "normal" a chance. You don't have to go all '50s housewife and move to the suburbs, but you might be surprised at the peace that a little stability can bring to your life.

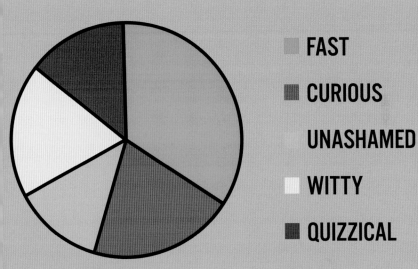

FAST

CURIOUS

UNASHAMED

WITTY

QUIZZICAL

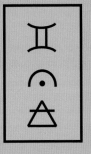

LIKES	DISLIKES
Starting rumors	Hearing about it last
Providing entertainment	Being bored
Sugar & caffeine	Decaf anything

SKILLS	STRUGGLES
Juggling tasks	Focusing on a single task
Finding the words	Sticking to a word limit
Keeping you informed	Deciding what to tell you

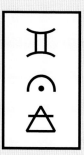

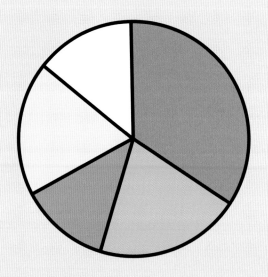

- ADAPTABLE
- IMAGINATIVE
- CURIOUS
- QUICK
- OPTIMISTIC

CAREER

You'll probably have several jobs or career pivots, plus side hustles. Who doesn't these days? You, however, may enjoy the flexibility more than others, who prefer to be more grounded in their calendar invites. You're just good at picking up new skills and synthesizing them, and then people pay you to do things. Somehow you've always got a guy (or girl) to connect you. Isn't that how this works? It is for you, anyway.

You need excitement and find repetition boring. You'd rather have your phone ringing off the hook than be tied to a desk pushing paper day after day. In fact, you don't mind being busy as long as you have company. If you want to play to your strengths, choose careers where communication is key. Think journalism, public relations, and education. No matter what field you choose, your focus on building relationships and making connections should remain at the heart of what you do.

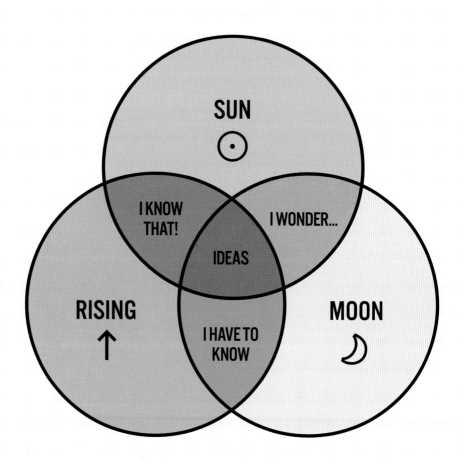

Speaking of that whole sun, moon, and rising thing—this is the outline of Gemini energy, but the energy manifests a little differently depending on where it shows up in your chart.

GEMINI SUN

Gemini suns are here to show the world how we communicate, how we develop ideas, how we *share* ideas—and also how we let them go. You are a font of the new, of absorbing and synthesizing new information all the time. This is what you're here to do: bring new ideas to new people. Follow-through is a different story, but you're full of inspiration. A Gemini sun is all about sparkling conversation and making connections. You might find yourself remarkably adept at introducing people to bring them together, and you can do the same with information. It's the process of following your curiosity that excites you, which ensures you're rarely bored, and often feel there's never enough time for everything you want to learn.

CHARISMATIC RESTLESS
INTELLIGENT DISTRACTED

GEMINI MOON

What makes you feel emotionally safe? Heard? Valued? Talking about it. Words of affirmation. A new book never went awry. When your moon is in Gemini, you have a fundamental need to express your feelings verbally. This is the quintessential "let's talk it out" placement—or maybe, "let's talk around every issue." You need the people you care about to share their feelings and to be able to share yours to feel safe. But if people try to pin you down, you can feel like you're in a cage. It's important to communicate your needs and expectations.

INTERESTING · MOODY
FRIENDLY · CONFUSING

GEMINI RISING

With your rising sign in airy Gemini, you relate to others in a distinctly open-minded way. You are less interested in getting things right than you are in hearing new perspectives. You are happiest when you're learning new things. Your eyes light up at the mention of an unfamiliar topic or a new trend. Your fascination with every nook and cranny of human existence can come off as gossipy, but it's rarely from a place of ill will. You just find humanity genuinely riveting and can't help but share.

Whatever your sun sign is, the Gemini rising means you're passionate about *communicating* that vision in the world. You're charming AF and very good at turning it on (you know *exactly* what we mean), even if you're an introvert at heart. You're witty with a deep appreciation for banter and people who are on your level when it comes to humor and juggling a million topics at once.

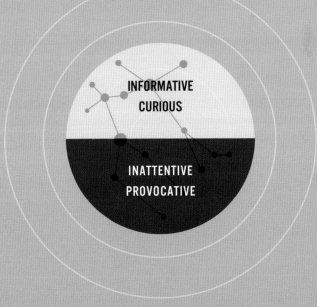

INFORMATIVE
CURIOUS

INATTENTIVE
PROVOCATIVE

TAKE CARE!	I MADE U A SNACK	MADE IT MYSELF	SALT LYFE	#COZY
WANT SOME TEA?	FUR BABIES	WANNA TALK?	SNIP SNIP	I CAN HELP
WANNA PLAY?	NO THANKS	Free	NEW PET NAMES	BAKING CHAMP
I'LL FIX IT	WINE O'CLOCK	LET'S GO HOME	I HAD A FEELING	MADE UR FAVE
SNUGGLES	SECRET FREAK	BEAR HUGS	I THOUGHT SO	PULL A CARD

Cancer

DATES	ELEMENT	MODALITY
June 21–July 22	Water	Cardinal

We never know what depths await simply by looking at the surface, especially when we're looking at you, Cancer. Your sign is represented by the crab and ruled by the moon (a.k.a. celestial ruler of Big Feelings). It is the manifestation of the common sense saying, "Never judge a book by its cover." In your case, you may present a tough exterior to the outside world, but at your core, you are incredibly emotionally intelligent, empathetic, and generous.

As the cardinal water sign, you initiate a paradigm shift from the influence of breezy air sign Gemini to the more intense, internal, emotional realm that you and your fellow water signs (Scorpio and Pisces) inhabit. Where others might fill space with small talk, you take in the world around you and feel your way through life. You nurture the insights you gather from daily life and transform this knowledge into illuminated wisdom.

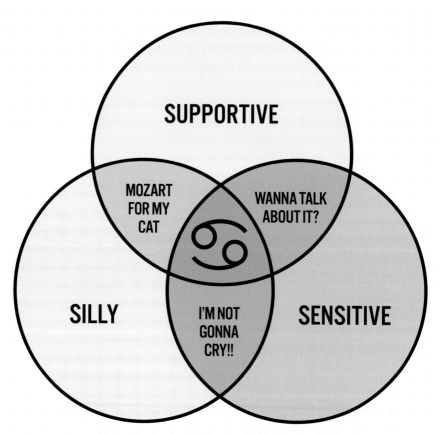

You have a brilliant imagination, and it's almost spooky how perceptive you can be. To casual acquaintances, you could come off as stoic or intimidating at times, when in fact, you are one of the most sensitive and loving signs in the zodiac. It can feel impossible to live in this world with a heart as open as yours, but don't retreat into your shell, Cancer. Follow the guidance of your intuition. Take the alone time you need to process. If you listen to your body and make time to fill your own cup, you will be able to freely pour your love into everything you do.

You truly shine when you are in your own safe space, surrounded by people you care about. The next time you host a gathering, pay special attention to the light in your friends' faces. Listen to their easy laughter. Know that you are the warm hearth that others gather around when they want to feel comfortable and safe. You are the first call a friend makes when they need a shoulder to cry on. Far from being a fair-weather friend, you are devoted to those who you love. People in your life count on you to show up on the stormiest nights of the soul, and you rarely disappoint.

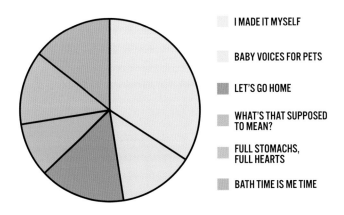

I MADE IT MYSELF

BABY VOICES FOR PETS

LET'S GO HOME

WHAT'S THAT SUPPOSED TO MEAN?

FULL STOMACHS, FULL HEARTS

BATH TIME IS ME TIME

As a child, you were more likely to dole out this devotion freely to everyone and anyone. You weren't born guarding your heart; you learned to protect yourself after experiences made you feel taken advantage of or unappreciated. You are not wrong to be protective, but here's the thing—the world might mistake your soft heart for weakness, but that is a misunderstanding of your gifts. Your strength is not in spite of your tenderness; your strength is derived from your deep capacity for love.

RELATIONSHIPS

In romantic relationships, you can be hard to get. It takes a special person to lower the walls that guard your heart. Once you let that special someone in, you are loyal, attentive, and always looking for opportunities to demonstrate your love. When you are feeling safe and balanced, you create the perfect environment for love to bloom. You are oriented toward deep bonding, and you need a partner that shares this drive for intimacy. If you are still looking for that person, it is important to practice being vulnerable and open early on in the relationship, which will be challenging, but it's worth it in the long run. If you are partnered, it is important to give your partner space. With your love of giving love, you might find yourself smothering your partner, especially if they are not used to being taken care of.

The key for you is healthy boundaries. Your empathetic nature can lead to over-identifying with your partner's feelings and losing yourself in the process. The tricky bit is that it can feel so good to lose yourself in another person that relationships can become a priority to the exclusion of everything else. You'll need to regularly ask yourself: How do I feel? What do I need? Communicate the answers to these questions to your partner. The right person will be happy to reciprocate your generosity by honoring your boundaries.

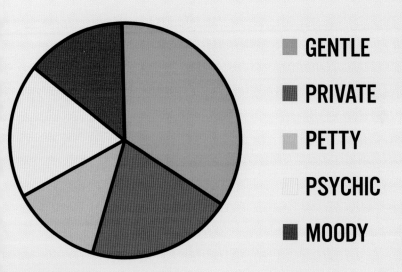

GENTLE

PRIVATE

PETTY

PSYCHIC

MOODY

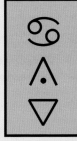

LIKES	DISLIKES
Uninterrupted cuddling	Side hugs
Homemade anything	Bad vibes
Being asked	Secrets

SKILLS	STRUGGLES
Cultivating talents	Nurturing a grudge
Sensitive to others	Overwhelmed by chaos
Going with the flow	Getting swept up in the flow

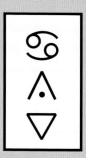

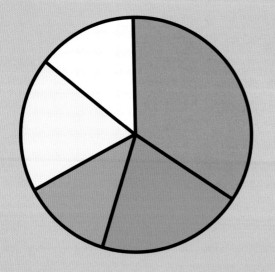

- INTUITIVE
- NURTURING
- ORGANIZED
- TRUSTWORTHY
- CARING

CAREER

All of your intuitive genius and your dedication to things you care about will serve you well in your career. You thrive in an atmosphere that leaves you ample time for unconventional problem solving, quiet reflection, and yes, even daydreaming. Your ideal career offers stability and ample opportunities for creativity. When you have what you need, you are pragmatic, careful, and let your intuition guide your strategy.

While you're swimming through the deep water of your imagination at work, observers might think you're procrastinating—wrong again, outsiders! No matter how much you like your work and your coworkers, your process works best when it's quiet and internal. The brass tacks? A daily work schedule full of meetings, watercooler convos about the weather, and open-floor workspaces are the bane of your existence. Lucky for you, Cancer, you have a secret weapon. Like the crab that carries its home on its back, you can bring the peace of mind and serenity you feel in your own safe space with you into the world (even while you're sitting in through a marathon of Monday meetings). If you feel overwhelmed or checked-out in your career, take long, deep breaths and engage your sense of touch. Think of the way a baby is instantly calmed when they get a hold of their blanket. Find your inconspicuous version of a baby blanket to bring you back down to earth. Grounding your energy in your work life is a top priority to keep you from burning out.

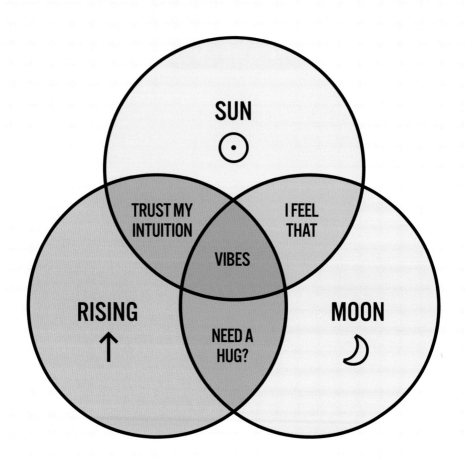

Cancer's emotional depth and deep-seated need to be cozy manifests in different ways depending on which planets in your chart land in Cancer. Your sun, moon, and rising signs point to the nuanced ways Cancer's energy turns up in your personality.

CANCER SUN

If your sun sign is in Cancer, your soul's major aspiration is to master the powerful tides of your emotional sea and use your gifts with discernment. The challenge for you is to learn how and when to protect your sensitive heart so that you can use your gifts at the right time. Conserve your energy without freezing up or freezing others out. Open up to those around you without giving everything away. That may sound like a tall order, but practice these skills in little ways in your daily life. You'll know that you're on the right path when you come home from a long day and don't immediately collapse on the couch, close your eyes, and shut out the world.

IMAGINATIVE MOODY
WELCOMING SUSPICIOUS

CANCER MOON

The moon rules Cancer, so if this is the moon's placement in your chart, the archetypal qualities of both are amplified in your psyche and in your emotional body. People with their moon in Cancer love to be at home engaging in nurturing, nourishing activities like cooking, eating, and pursuing their hobbies alone or with close friends and family. With such a sensitive nature, you run the risk of moodiness and lashing out when you're out of whack. Grounding, embodied practices, and ample alone time are needed.

NURTURING INSECURE
PROTECTIVE MARTYR

CANCER RISING

If Cancer is your rising sign, the first impression you make on people can either be one of a nurturing, gentle, maternal type, or an edgy, aloof type—it all depends on whether or not you're taking good care of yourself and feeling safe or overly exposed. You prefer depth and honest connection over surface-level banter. Some might find you a tad standoffish, but you just keep your cards close to your chest. Even if you're not the type to open up right away, you adapt to new environments easily and can make others feel at home no matter where you are.

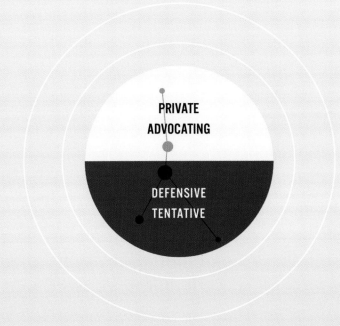

PRIVATE
ADVOCATING

DEFENSIVE
TENTATIVE

STATEMENT CLOTHES	HAPPY HOUR!	SHADES ON	AN URGE TO CREATE	PERSONALITY QUIZZES
NEW CRUSHES	WEARING GOLD	DYED HAIR	IMPULSE SHOPPING	IT'S "ME" SEASON
BE ORIGINAL	DON'T BE SHY	Free	JUST DO IT	HEY, LOOK AT ME.
LOVE LETTERS	BINGING MOVIES	WATCHING SUNSETS	CROPPED T-SHIRTS	KEEPIN' IT REAL
INSPIRED BY EVERYTHING	I'M BORED	XOXO	THAT'S WILD	DRESS TO IMPRESS

♌Leo

DATES	ELEMENT	MODALITY
July 23–August 22	Fire	Fixed

When you are as luminous as the sun, people are going to notice you, Leo. They can't help it! Anybody's eye would be caught by the shiniest object in the room, and in any room you enter, that eye-catching shimmer is more than likely emanating from you. Represented by the lion and ruled by the star at the center of our solar system, you are a natural leader. Make no mistake, you are not the zodiac's middle manager—you were born under the particular celestial alignment that places a crown on your head and puts courage in your heart.

As the fixed sun sign ruled by the sun itself, you possess boundless creativity and a fundamental drive to share your inspiration with others. In this way, Leo, you take the wisdom gathered during the emotional and introverted Cancer season and turn it into treasure—into something that everyone wants a piece of. If Cancer raises the wheat and bakes the bread, you are the one to invite the whole town to the feast and pass out the loaves.

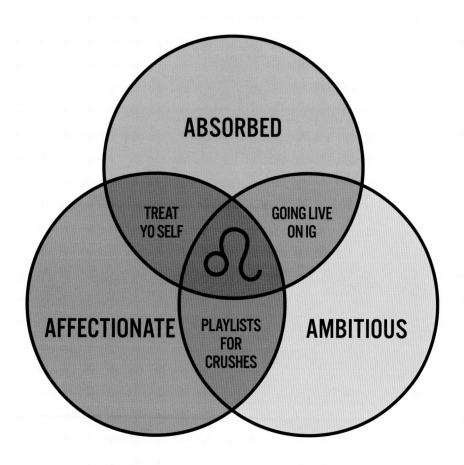

Under the influence of your ruling star, you are used to drawing others into your orbit. Warm, charming, and quick to laugh, any room you walk into is captivated by your light. You love to surprise and thrill others. You love parties, live music, and bustling streets. You love meeting new people and catching up with old friends. It might be quicker to put it this way—you are in love with life. Your love is not simple or superficial; it is dynamic and pours out of the deepest place in your heart. You excite those with big, adventurous personalities. You lend your courage to those who need it and inspire bravery in them.

Although you are represented by the lion, "ferocious" is not quite the right word to describe you. You have more of the demeanor of a cuddly, playful cat who just happens to be larger than life. You have a childlike quality that delights in attention, praise, and reward. You move through the world like a lion moves with its pride, feeling not-quite-right in the world unless you are surrounded by others. After all, if there is no one to see your latest dazzling feat, did it even happen? One of the keys to unlocking your full potential, Leo, is to accept that you are dazzling even without anyone there to admire you.

When you are alone with yourself and feeling out of balance, you crave that pack mentality. You can ignore the inner voice that makes you feel like you are not worthy of the love you receive, or that you are nothing without other people. Chasing love and adoration this way can still leave you hollow if it's only to appease your desire for validation. Every Leo's biggest secret is that underneath the glitter and jokes, there is a creeping sense of incompletion. Once you're aware of it, you can learn to be your own audience.

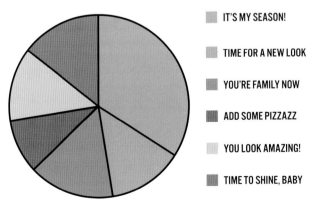

IT'S MY SEASON!

TIME FOR A NEW LOOK

YOU'RE FAMILY NOW

ADD SOME PIZZAZZ

YOU LOOK AMAZING!

TIME TO SHINE, BABY

If you ever find that you've fallen too deeply in love with yourself or obsessed with your latest crush, your confidence can twist into arrogance. Your vast capacity for love can get caught up in the ego and fixate on fleeting pleasures. Luckily for a pleasure-seeker like yourself, the cure is not self-denial or punishment. Instead of intensely focusing on a narrow pursuit, redirect your energy toward a broadly altruistic feeling of love for all people. This is how you earn that crown you were born with. You see, the difference between a neurotic Leo and a healthy Leo is simple. A wounded, anxious Leo charms the pants off other people to prove to themselves that they are lovable. A healthy, regal Leo brings joy to those around them because of a heartfelt desire to make people happy—no strings attached.

RELATIONSHIPS

In terms of your romantic life, you will never be without options. Wildly charming and always popular, you could leave any party with a pocket full of phone numbers if you want to. You enthrall potential love interests with your talent and charisma. There will be times in your life when you're happiest playing the field. After all, if one date is good, then five dates are better, right? Well, yes and no. There is a season for all Leos when this kind of exploration feels nourishing. There is also a season to explore more serious bonding with your chosen person. When you find someone who inspires you to commit, you'll find fulfillment in a way that no cheering crowd or grand prize can compare to. And once you find this treasure, you will guard it passionately. You are a loyal partner and you live to earn the favor of your beloved. Take care not to lose yourself in this pursuit. Remember to keep a balanced social schedule and spend time with friends and family, even if you are just craving the attention of that certain someone.

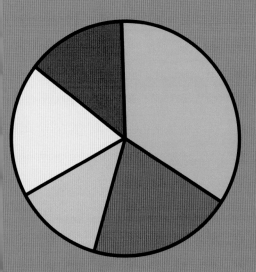

■ **PROUD**

■ **CREATIVE**

■ **SILLY**

■ **AFFECTIONATE**

■ **ENTERTAINING**

LIKES	DISLIKES
High praise	Being ignored
Good lighting	Bad angles
Loyalty	Fair-weather friends

SKILLS	STRUGGLES
Directing a team	Following directions
Creative solutions	Impulse control
Giving feedback	Applying feedback

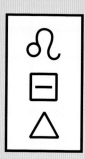

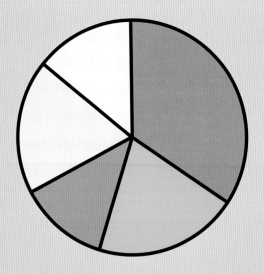

- TENACIOUS
- AMBITIOUS
- LOYAL
- BOLD
- GENEROUS

CAREER

As a born leader, you have many of the qualities that job listings love to include: highly motivated, excellent people skills, high energy—the list goes on. With your big public persona, you are seen as competitive, determined, and fun to be around at work. You sparkle in brainstorms. The deep well of your creativity seems bottomless. Your passion is magnetic, and colleagues can't wait to rally behind any cause you champion. You do your best work when you feel like other people are watching. Careers that reward your creativity, challenge you, and provide a kind of audience are ideal. You'll find fulfillment in the performing arts, in motivational work such as fitness training or life coaching, in politics, or in teaching roles.

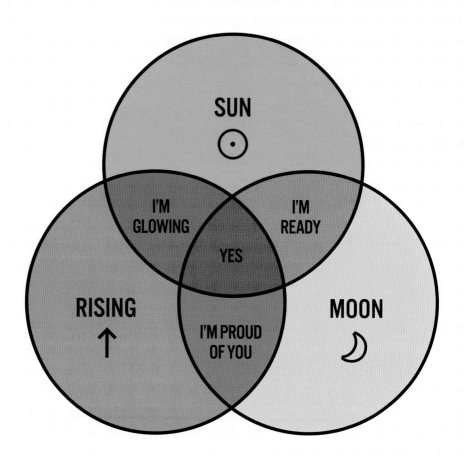

Phew! That was a lot, but we know it's hard to scare off a lion. Are you ready to go deeper, Leo? Your sun, moon, and rising sign shape the way Leo's energy manifests in different aspects of your life.

LEO SUN

The sun is the center of the solar system and likewise provides a center for the way that the different elements of our psyche organize to create our full personalities. In your case, the sun is also your ruling planet. This endows you with an innate charisma and that special x-factor that draws people to you. The most authentic and stable version of your personality is that of a regal leader who rules not from a place of ego but from a place of love. Strive to embody generosity and compassion whenever you feel your ego roaring in the background.

LOYAL BOASTFUL
AFFECTIONATE ARROGANT

LEO MOON

Your basic emotional life is joyful and confident. With the emotional moon in fiery Leo, your inner life can be intense and exhilarating, if a little dramatic. At times, you may struggle to find a balance between ecstatic intensity and a sense of dull emptiness. The key to maintaining a sense of calm and well-being is to find an outlet for your boundless energy. For many Leo moons, these outlets tend to be creative and especially performative, like dance or drama. Sports, marathons, or other competitive pursuits will also work wonders on your emotional self.

CREATIVE CHARISMATIC

DRAMATIC SELFISH

LEO RISING

One thing is certain if Leo is your rising sign—you are not an easy person to forget. You make a distinct impression on everyone you meet. People remember your warmth, your dramatic flair, and your infectious joy. You come across as playful and vivacious. If someone hands you a mic, you'll find something charming to say into it. You might not admit it, but as a Leo rising you will require tons of attention and praise. Luckily, you are naturally gifted and have a heart big enough to share.

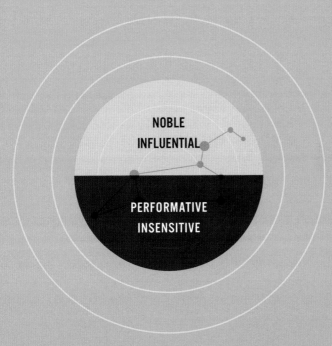

NOBLE
INFLUENTIAL

PERFORMATIVE
INSENSITIVE

I GOT IT	CHECK AGAIN	CRUSHING IT	COFFEE PLS	IN MY PLANNER
DND MODE	GARDENING	HOMEMADE	CHOREOGRAPHY	CHECKLISTS
CONTROL ISSUES	GROWTH	Free	#GOALS	THAT'S NOT PRACTICAL
BUDGET	LOVE NOTES	WORK HARD PLAY HARD	TOLD YOU SO	#BLESSED
DO IT AGAIN	MAHOGANY	I READ ABT THAT	I DON'T THINK SO	IT'S BC I CARE

Virgo

DATES	ELEMENT	MODALITY
August 23–September 22	Earth	Mutable

For you, Virgo, it's all about the details. Like the goddess of wheat and agriculture that represents your sign, your personality is rooted in the abundance of the earth. You are attuned to the natural laws and order of the world we live in. As the mutable earth sign, Virgo weathers every season of life with a grounded sense of ease. How you do the small things—attentively—is how you do everything. You know that winter always turns to spring. During the darker times in life, you put your head down and attend to the work in front of you to sustain yourself and your loved ones. You love a daily routine, and a good day to you is when you fit every activity into its assigned time slot.

Governed by Mercury, both your sign and Gemini are focused on communication, but your two approaches could not be more different. Where Gemini is focused on being seen and understood by others, Virgo prefers to perceive the

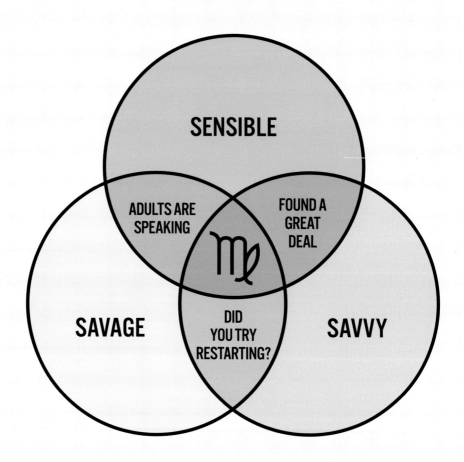

world, to soak up all the words and colors and feelings and sounds that the world has to offer, processing this information at their own pace and reporting back only the carefully curated insights. This careful, active listening is the standout quality of this sign.

You're an incredibly sensitive person who is more likely to listen than you are to speak. This orientation drives your success in areas of your life that move in a straight line: finishing school, running a quadrathlon (or whatever is harder than a triathlon), finding a job, and absolutely crushing it. Sure, you like to win—maybe not as much as Aries or Capricorn, but still, it feels good. What's more important than winning for you, Virgo? Say it with us: perfection.

Whoever the first person to be called a perfectionist was, they were probably a Virgo. This, of course, is a trait that causes a lot of unnecessary suffering, because as we know, nobody's perfect. Remember that people are not projects, Virgo, and that includes yourself. It is beautiful that you are always striving to be better than you were yesterday, but you do not have to be constantly perfecting yourself in order to be loved, valued, and whole. You're worthy and wonderful in the present moment, too!

Your astrological precedent Leo, ruled by the sun, illuminates the world from above. You use that light to see the world more clearly, and since Virgo season is all about being able to separate the wheat from the chaff (do you see what we did there?), a little overhead lighting is a must. Once you're done winnowing all those imperfections, Libra's airy energy breezes through, seeking to put everything in balance. Speaking of balance, has anyone ever told you anything along the lines of "work hard, play hard"? If not, allow us to be the first. You need to kick back on occasion and embrace some flaws so that you can balance all your effort with rest and decompression.

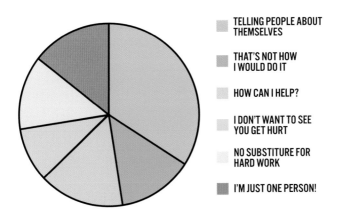

- TELLING PEOPLE ABOUT THEMSELVES
- THAT'S NOT HOW I WOULD DO IT
- HOW CAN I HELP?
- I DON'T WANT TO SEE YOU GET HURT
- NO SUBSTITUTE FOR HARD WORK
- I'M JUST ONE PERSON!

You're a natural helper with a generous, loving heart. Make sure to regularly put yourself at the top of your priority list and get back some of the love you give out.

RELATIONSHIPS

Speaking of love, you can be a hard nut to crack. Virgos need to feel safe to open up and demonstrate all their mushy feelings. You have to be sure that the energy you put into a relationship will be worth your time. You want to take your time in love and make careful choices about who you open your heart to, and when. Once you open up, though, you're a devoted partner. Virgos prefer stability to spontaneous flings. With a fling, they never get to see their vulnerability rewarded and transformed into deep intimacy. Highly methodical, you have every relationship all mapped out in your head, and at times you can seem as if you're trying to analyze your partner. You want to know if they will fit into the role you dreamed up for them. If Virgo rules the relationship area of your chart, you'll spend a lot of energy looking for the right person. It's important to separate the fantasy of who your partner is from reality. No relationship is perfect, Virgo, but love is worth the risk of failure.

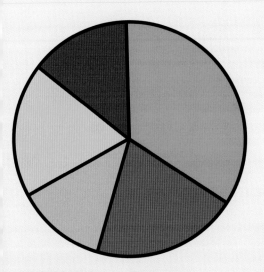

■ PRACTICAL

■ HARD WORKING

■ CRITICAL

■ CORRECT

■ HELPFUL

LIKES	DISLIKES
When things work	Chaos
An itinerary	Stupidity
Devotion	Being taken for granted

SKILLS	STRUGGLES
Knowing what you need	Asking for what they need
Establishing routines	Being flexible
Cultivating efficiency	Cultivating perfectionism

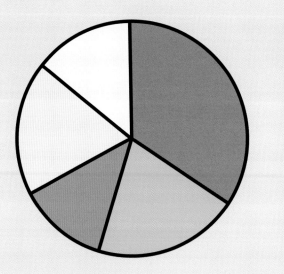

■ PERSISTENT

■ WELL-INFORMED

■ PRACTICED

■ THOUGHTFUL

■ HELPFUL

CAREER

As the ultimate sign of earthly order, Virgos shine in all matters of practicality, analysis, and follow-through. Your organized way of looking at the world is a high-value skill in any career that deals with complex systems, problem-solving, and clear, concise thought. Virgo's inherent aptitude for dealing with the material world also makes you very good with your hands. You can turn blueprints into skyscrapers (metaphorically and literally—lots of excellent Virgo architects in the history books!). You're a superstar when it comes to saving money. You demonstrate an iron will with your personal budgets and excel at saying "no" to frivolous spending. The growth point here for you, Virgo, is to learn to indulge more in the things that give you pleasure outside of work and to take more risks professionally. What would you do if you knew you couldn't fail? Get after it!

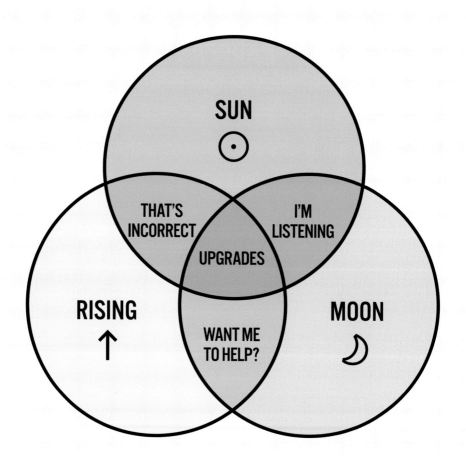

Always in search of completion, finish off your Virgo crash course by learning about Virgo sun, moon, and rising signs. The sun is the core of your personality. The position of the moon influences our emotional instincts and what we need to feel nurtured, while your rising sign is the mask you wear for the world.

VIRGO SUN

Wherever the sun shines in your chart is the place you go to find direction during rudderless moments in life. The sun is our compass; it is who we fundamentally are meant to be. Solar Virgos' lives are oriented toward the careful orchestration of life's finer details to create a healthy, beautiful whole. They don't enforce their ideas of perfection by being bossy or manipulative. Instead, it's in their nature to be persuasive, measured, and logical. You see the best in humanity. You value the simple things in life. You love a schedule and a plan, so sudden deviation from your plan can cause a mini-meltdown. To grow into Virgo's highest form, you need to focus your energy on serving others and practicing loads of self-forgiveness.

DEVOTED CRITICAL
PRACTICAL ANXIOUS

VIRGO MOON

For lunar Virgos, contentedness comes from feeling in control of all the chaotic little details of daily life like paying bills, grocery shopping, making their annual trip to the dentist for a teeth cleaning, etc. If your moon is in Virgo, you are happiest when you know that you feel helpful and appreciated. Not an attention hog, you get your kicks from taking a backstage role. You can be skeptical and can't help yourself when it comes to pushing other people's buttons, especially if those buttons are illogical. You are excellent at pinpointing others' needs and tending to them. Lunar Virgos are kind, empathetic, and sometimes a bit shy. How to break the ice with a Virgo moon? Try asking them what they think is the best way to get from point A to point B, and they'll open right up.

CALM CAUTIOUS
ANALYTICAL COLD

VIRGO RISING

If your rising sign is Virgo, you come off as sharp and reserved. Tending toward shyness, you take your time processing the world around you. Some might read you as standoffish, but you just take a little longer to warm up than others. Once you're comfortable, you possess a quiet charm that draws people to you, especially people that need help. You love a fixer-upper, and as long as you know this about yourself and set clear boundaries, you can do a lot of good. Rising Virgos are easily distracted by small things that seem out of place. An attentive friend, you are the kind of person that never fails to tuck in your friend's tag or to casually pick lint off someone's shoulder. Sometimes, we all need a Virgo rising in our lives to tell us we have spinach in our teeth.

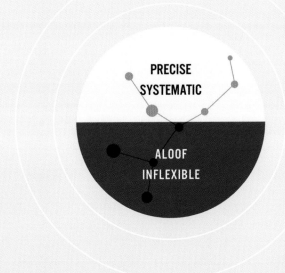

PRECISE
SYSTEMATIC

ALOOF
INFLEXIBLE

THAT'S PRETTY		NOT FAIR	GOT A CRUSH	SUGAR & SPICE
BEAUTY TIPS	I GOTCHU	MAKEOVER	MIND IF I...?	#BALANCE
ONLINE SHOPPING	CALLIGRAPHY	Free	PARTY!	JUST A SMIDGE
HYDRATE!	MAKING ART	POWER MATCHING	SILKS	MUSEUM TRIPS
INSTANT KARMA	WHO'S THAT?	PUTTIN' ON MOVES	KEEP THE PEACE	NICE TO MEET YOU

Libra

DATES	ELEMENT	MODALITY
September 23–October 22	Air	Cardinal

Libra, the cardinal air sign represented by the scales, signifies the basic drive for balance in all aspects of their life. For Libra, justice and balance are beauty, and beauty is the highest good. Venus, the planet that governs love, beauty, and money, rules this sign. Those with Libra in their chart display an obvious affinity for all the things that sparkle. As a matter of fact, "sparkle" might be a good word to describe you in general. You also have the ability to see any issue or idea from all sides and find just the right words to reach consensus and harmony. You could charm the birds out of the trees, and you transform breakdowns in communication into breakthroughs.

Libra is about polish and sophistication. You love a color-coordinated closet, elevated aesthetics, and a dose of high art. Your ideal day would include wearing your favorite outfit, dining at the chicest spot for small plates, and strolling

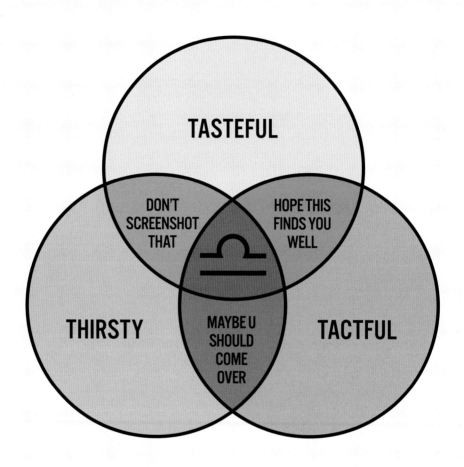

through museums while taking ample breaks to pontificate over cappuccinos with your companion. Each sign is associated with a body part and for Libra, that's the skin, which makes sense. The skin is the surface of the body and Libra is entranced by the surface of things. Think Narcissus falling in love with his reflection on the surface of a pond. And hey, Libra does indeed love a shiny surface (mirrors, for example).

The absolute biggest flirt in the zodiac, Libra would flirt with your ex, your future ex, your fourth cousin, and the cute stranger on the train. More often than not, you don't mean anything more than the flirtation; you just love the music of a playful conversation and the thrill of connection. Also big on people-pleasing, it is your first instinct to give others what they want. It can be hard for you to distinguish between your needs and feelings and the needs and feelings of other people.

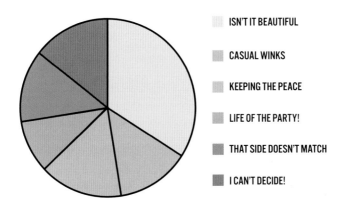

- ISN'T IT BEAUTIFUL
- CASUAL WINKS
- KEEPING THE PEACE
- LIFE OF THE PARTY!
- THAT SIDE DOESN'T MATCH
- I CAN'T DECIDE!

As the cardinal air sign, you initiate the movement from detail-oriented, earthbound Virgo into expansive intellectualism. Your opposite sign, Aries, initiates a new astrological cycle with strong me-centered energy. By the time the wheel of the zodiac reaches Libra season, the energy has evolved into we-centered energy. You take all the lessons of the signs that precede you and apply their wisdom to relationships.

RELATIONSHIPS

We've arrived at Libra's favorite topic! Libra is all about relationships and is, arguably, the most romantic sign in the sky. Highly idealistic, Libra sees the best in everyone. That alone would be a charming trait, but Libra elevates this by helping others see the best in themselves. Although Libra loves to be in love, this arena can also present some challenges for the celestial scales. The duality of Libra's nature means that they can feel like they're finding their soulmate every time, even on a marathon of speed dates. Libra is a people-pleaser, and because they are so good at it, almost anyone can fall in love with them.

Idealistic Libra loves to be adored and might fall into the trap of believing that if someone is in love with them, then they must be soulmates. The trick to finding fulfilling relationships for Libra is to practice discernment. This means saying "no" to others and saying "yes" to yourself more. More self-care, fewer occasions for flattery. When Libra finds the balance between self and others, there's no sweeter love.

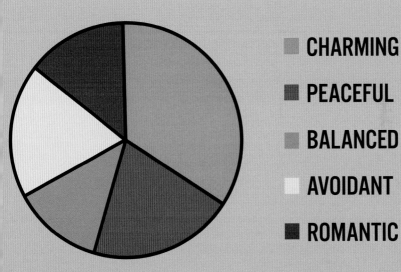

- **CHARMING**
- **PEACEFUL**
- **BALANCED**
- **AVOIDANT**
- **ROMANTIC**

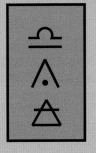

LIKES	DISLIKES
Flirting	Talking about the weather
Poetic confessions	Injustice
Chocolates (50% Cacao)	Bad taste

SKILLS	STRUGGLES
Mediating conflict	Stirring up conflict
Public relations	Office "relations"
Curating the look	Picking a final logo

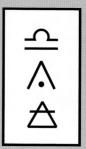

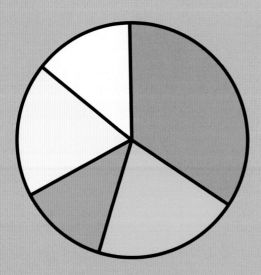

- POISED
- DIPLOMATIC
- FAIR
- ACCOMMODATING
- DELIBERATE

CAREER

Libra is never lacking in the imagination department. You want Libra on your team for any brainstorming sesh; they are excellent facilitators and love to find the middle ground between disparate ideas. If you are doing something you care about while surrounded by interesting people, you'll have a hard time heading home at the end of the day. Libra is so driven by bringing harmony and beauty into the world through making connections that they can become enchanted by their own ideas. Libra stays busy. If you have work planets placed in Libra, you need a lot of freedom to thrive. You wilt under micromanagement, but you do need some accountability buddies. Business is about relationships with Libra, and you need to strike the right balance between talking about all your big ideas and doing the day-to-day work that will make them a reality. It's not that you're careless; you're just more focused on the big picture than the details.

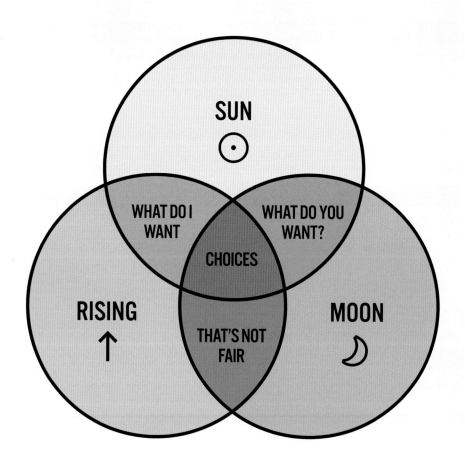

Libra loves balance and harmony, but that can mean different things depending on which planets enter the scales' domain of influence. Read about the sun, moon, and rising Libra qualities to learn about the finer points (we know you love finer things, Libra!).

LIBRA SUN

When the sun appears in Libra, you're driven by the need to make the world a fairer place. As the cardinal air sign, you will want to spend less time thinking about your ideals and more time making decisive action. Although Libra has a bad rap for taking way too long to choose which restaurant to go to, every Libra sun's compass always points toward balance, and balance can be hard to find. Speaking of trajectory, another of life's motivations for you is to find a companion to build a life with. You thrive when you have close relationships that allow you to be your best self because sometimes it is easier for you to receive love when you give love.

CHARMING VAIN
PEACEFUL INDECISIVE

LIBRA MOON

Your moon placement is all about your emotional experience, and it indicates what makes you feel emotionally safe. For lunar Libras, this generally means partnership. This is a moon of instant best friends, serial monogamists, and sister/brother/daughter/parent of the year. The moon also influences how you seek to understand others and how you want to be understood. You read people well, and you're excellent at showing people the side of yourself that they most want to see. This can become an emotional defense mechanism to avoid the vulnerability of revealing who you really are. You're diplomatic and tactful with everyone you meet, but with your partner or close friends, you can tend to lean into arguments just because you like to try on different perspectives. The lunar Libra is on a constant search for the very best of all possible worlds which can lead to some heartache, but take heart! When you let people see who you are, you'll realize there was nothing to hide.

DIPLOMATIC ANXIOUS
CHARMING WISHY-WASHY

LIBRA RISING

Your rising sign shapes the way you're perceived by others, and in your case, that perception is dazzling. People are attracted and enthralled by your way with words. An incorrigible flirt, you treat the art of charming others like a sport (a sport you're very good at by the way!), always making compromises or negotiating for the best possible outcome. You pay attention to the way you present yourself and you have a distinct sense of style. You surround yourself with beauty, and people can't help but want to be in the circle of light you cast. You can be so polished in your external presentation that people have a hard time imagining what you're like behind closed doors.

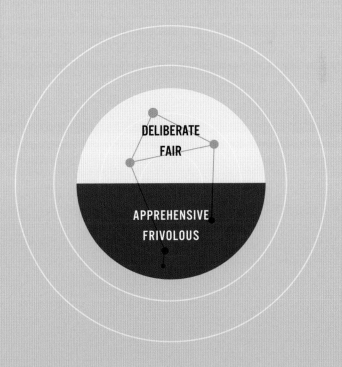

DELIBERATE
FAIR

APPREHENSIVE
FRIVOLOUS

I'LL NEVER TELL	*EYE CONTACT*	STAY AWAY!	COME BACK!	IN THE DEEP
FIGHT UR DEMONS	RAGE	TOO MANY FEELS	COFFEE, BLACK	NO THANKS
MAGNETIC AF	SWEET NOTHINGS	**Free**	STOP STEREOTYPING!	I BELIVE IN YOU
NIGHT TIME	EVERYTHING DIES	I LIKE PINK TOO	UR OBSESSED	KISS ME
GOD(DESS) OF DEATH	BE BRAVE	SHHH	*WHISPERS*	EW UR GROSS

Scorpio

DATES	ELEMENT	MODALITY
October 23–November 21	Water	Fixed

Scorpio is internet-famous for being a little intense, and you have to admit, the internet might have a point here. You are determined to follow your instincts and get what you want. You are fundamentally drawn to and motivated by power. Scorpios tend to be more intimidating than intimidated no matter who or what they are up against. However, Scorpio has the heart of a lover and a healer, not a fighter. You have a deeply romantic mystique that people can't stop talking about. Everyone wants to know what your secret is.

While Libra is all about creating surface-level harmony and charming small talk, Scorpio's energy is oriented toward a more primal experience. Drawing upon deep emotional and psychic strength, Scorpio turns inward to find meaning. Where other signs would shrink away, they show us how to face the darker side of life. This makes them excellent friends in hard times and the kind of person you want on your side (as well as someone you don't want to cross).

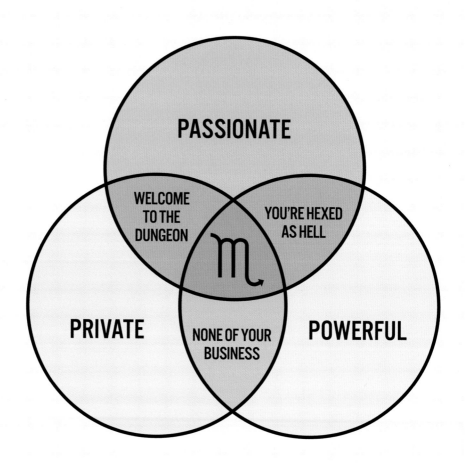

Ruled by Mars and Pluto, the planets of sexuality and power, Scorpio's energy is about death and rebirth. You are tapped into the mysteries that bookend either side of our lives, and you bring that otherworldly awareness to your relationships. As the fixed water sign, you take the introspective, emotionally profound work that cardinal Cancer initiates and make sure this energy is sustained. Bringing these elements together, Scorpio knows how to honor the sacred power of transformation.

You feel everything deeply, and we do mean *everything*. Physical, emotional, and mental, both pleasure and pain—all are worth experiencing to you because of the lessons each state teaches about our shared humanity. You are a healer, an alchemist, a person who can transform poison into medicine. You show us the interplay between shadow and light—the other side of grief is love, anger masks our vulnerability, and fear can be a cover for softness.

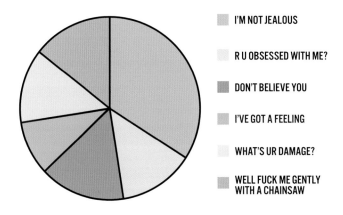

I'M NOT JEALOUS

R U OBSESSED WITH ME?

DON'T BELIEVE YOU

I'VE GOT A FEELING

WHAT'S UR DAMAGE?

WELL FUCK ME GENTLY WITH A CHAINSAW

You have a piercing intellect that immediately identifies the root of the matter at hand. You look at problems as puzzles and can be obsessive when it comes to finding solutions. You never shy away from getting your hands dirty in all areas of your life. Once you've committed to something, good luck to anyone who stands in your way. You're equally unafraid of messy convos about secret feelings as you are about moving to a new city and starting over. Your ability to go to the extreme in life is a strength and a challenge. Let this power overtake you, and you'll find yourself ricocheting from ecstasy to agony. Harness this power and there's nothing you can't have.

RELATIONSHIPS

Don't take this the wrong way, but if you wanted to become a cult leader, Scorpio, we have no doubt you could accomplish it. It's just that your particular intensity draws people to you and holds them there. You make people feel like they're the only one in the room when you speak to them. You make people feel like no one has ever understood them as deeply as you do. You are focused and dedicated in your method of love. When you've found the right person, you are quick to commit. You want to feel everything at its highest level of intensity, so you waste no time with the superficial elements.

You can be possessive, but when you're self-aware and setting healthy boundaries, you manage to keep this quality in check. Jealousy is also a common affliction among Scorpios in love. You're looking for a partner that isn't put off by your intensity and who recognizes the courage it requires to feel everything so deeply. When you find that person, a Scorpio's love can be transformative and healing. You're not put off by the moments in life that other people find awkward or embarrassing. You don't think twice about dropping everything to be there for your loved ones. Your love is a treasure, and don't you forget it!

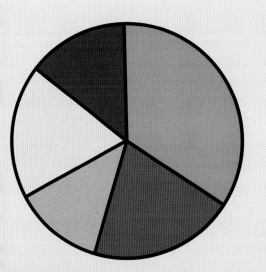

- **POWERFUL**
- **MAGNETIC**
- **SENSUAL**
- **DRAMATIC**
- **BRAVE**

LIKES	DISLIKES
Sweet vengeance	Repression
Dramatic professions	Simplicity
A glass of red	Reasons to be jealous

SKILLS	STRUGGLES
Finding out the truth	Letting it go
Staying calm	Keeping it casual
Clear communication	Using a filter

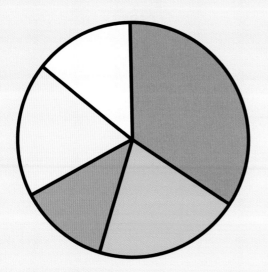

RESILIENT

HONEST

FOCUSED

CAPTIVATING

PERCEPTIVE

CAREER

In the working world, Scorpio is self-motivated, passionate, and definitely not a quitter. Confident to the extreme, Scorpio walks into any situation as if they were born for it. With your affinity for all the hidden and mysterious elements of life, you are excellent at solving problems that others haven't even identified yet. You're known around the office for working late and arriving early because once you're engaged in a project, your drive can be all-consuming. But you hate busy work and struggle to stay motivated if you're not being adequately challenged. You need to be in a position that allows you to plunge into complexity and get lost in the web of information. People tend to confess to you. It's like you're walking around with a neon sign over your head that says, "I can keep a secret." This is a huge advantage in the career world, and you must be strategic with this and all your many gifts.

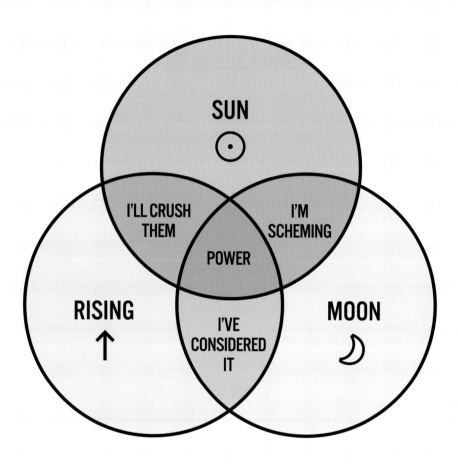

Depth is your specialty, Scorpio, so why not dig a bit deeper into the influence of the sun, moon, and rising sign in your chart? Your sun sign shows your core personality and growth points, the moon shapes your emotional landscape, and your rising sign is the face you show to others.

SCORPIO SUN

If your sun is in Scorpio, your path through life is laid out in the unusual trio of creatures that represents your sign. Although usually represented by the scorpion, your sign actually has two other symbols associated with it (of course, leave it to Scorpio to have even more hidden depths!). The eagle and the phoenix both also represent the ways your energy can be transformed. At the beginning of your development, you stay low as a scorpion to the ground and keep to the shadowy places where you're comfortable. You hide from the sun and strike out of fear. The eagle takes a higher perspective, moves with grace, and experiences freedom while diving down to strike only when appropriate. The phoenix is the mythic creature who bursts into flame and is reborn from ashes, illustrating that at your highest level of self-realization, you are absolute magic.

PASSIONATE OBSESSIVE
DEVOTED INTENSE

SCORPIO MOON

The placement of the moon in your chart determines your emotional landscape and defines what you need to feel secure. When you're a Scorpio moon, this inner world is mysterious terrain. At your best, you're the definition of the words "passion," "depth," and "wisdom." You're the friend everyone needs during our hardest times. One of the greatest gifts lunar Scorpios give the world is their understanding of the shadows. You never shy away from the darker side of life, but you learn from the valleys and carry insights back up to the surface. You heal yourself and others through inner exploration and through learning to surrender control. Your emotional depth and intensity can become destructive if it is not balanced with gratitude and grace.

INTUITIVE SECRETIVE
STRONG MANIPULATIVE

SCORPIO RISING

Your rising sign is the mask you wear to face the world. If your rising sign is in Scorpio, we would be hard-pressed to find someone who comes off with more raw, magnetic energy than you do. You know how some people walk in a room and you can't stop looking at them—there's just this kind of sparkle? That person may very well be a Scorpio rising. You often become the center of gravity at any party, and the VIP section seems to form around you. Sexy and mysterious, everyone is begging to be let into your secret world. Though not loud or a show-off, you draw people to you with a reserved, powerful presence. However, no one wants to be on your bad side. You are a fascinating and passionate friend and an equally passionate enemy.

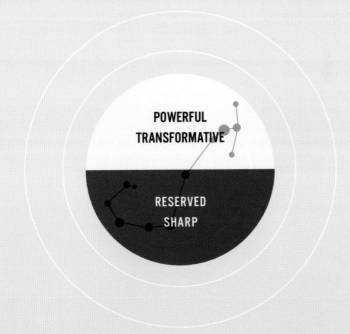

POWERFUL
TRANSFORMATIVE

RESERVED
SHARP

GOTTA GO	BOLD AF	ON THE RUN	STAYING PRESENT	IT'LL BE OKAY!
ETHICS 101	LEARNING	DAD JOKES	READ THIS	FRESH AIR
WHAT'S SLEEP?	"WINK"	Free	OOO SHINY	TEAM TOO MUCH
CAFFEINATED	CRUNCH GRANOLA	BOHO-CHIC	NEW ERA PLS	LET'S DO IT!
MOVING ON NOW	I'LL TEXT YOU	WHY SO GRUMPY?	WHAT ARE RULES	WHOOPS, I FORGOT

Sagittarius

DATES	ELEMENT	MODALITY
November 22–December 21	Fire	Mutable

First of all, congratulations on settling down long enough to read your profile! This is no small feat for you, Sagittarius, as a sign that is always on the go. Optimistic and adventurous, you always prefer to be out in the world and living ferociously, rather than sitting still and planning out your days. Predictably, you're not a fan of routines or mundane schedules. Once you've done something, what's the point of doing it all over again the next day?

Represented by the archer, a half-man and half-horse centaur, Sagittarius is all about the interplay between our animal nature and the desire for spiritual transcendence. Sagittarian energy takes the introspective, deep, and sometimes dark insights of Scorpio with a grain of salt. You bring an easygoing joy to the serious business of living well. You see the darker sides of life thanks to moody Scorpio, but they spur you on to seek out new challenges and new friends to give yourself a sense of meaning.

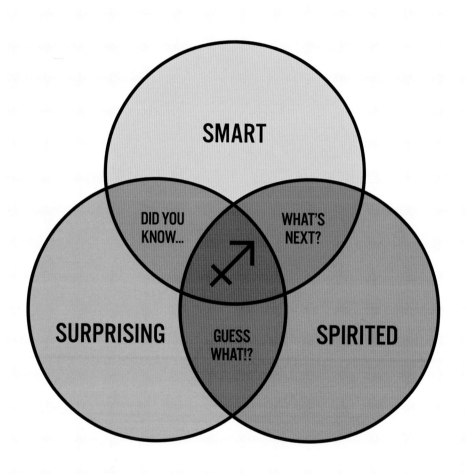

As a mutable fire sign, you embody the quick passion of your fiery brethren (Leo and Aries). However, your mutable modality makes you adaptable and equally quick to forgive and forget when something rankles you. Jupiter, your ruling planet, brings good luck, good vibes, and exciting opportunities. No wonder your sign is known for such a sunny disposition.

- OOPS I DID IT AGAIN!
- I PLAYED WITH YOUR HEART
- GOT LOST IN THE GAME
- THE GLASS IS HALF FULL
- FEELING LUCKY?
- CAN'T WIN IF YOU DON'T PLAY

You love to laugh and you're naturally inclined to believe in the goodness of all people and the world at large. You love to learn and you're quick to jump into things because you figure that, no matter what happens, you'll walk away with new information that will ultimately make you a better person. You can be a little flippant about big decisions and risks. If this were a high school yearbook, you'd be voted "Most Likely to Randomly Move to a New Country for Fun." Some more conservative signs might find you a little too whimsical or even irresponsible. But because of your direct, cheerful, and honest nature, it's really hard to stay mad at you!

RELATIONSHIPS

The ideal date for a Sagittarius? A hike to the top of an unassuming local hilltop only to find—surprise! A picnic basket full of assorted finger foods that Sag has never tried before. Then, you spend hours talking about your dreams and spirituality and languages you want to learn one day. This dream date encapsulates it all for Sag. Physical exertion? Check. Surprise? Check. Novel experiences? Check.

Love and intimacy for Sag are bound up with adventure, growth, and expansion. However, it's not all giggles and butterflies. You are a unique mix of joyful puppy energy and a restless desire to transcend the bounds of the everyday. This dichotomy between the playful pursuit of pleasure and serious contemplation of the meaning of life can be hard to grasp for new potential partners. You value your freedom and don't commit easily. You draw people to you with your humor and your enthusiasm. Loving a Sagittarius means loving the great unknown and finding the courage to grow in new directions.

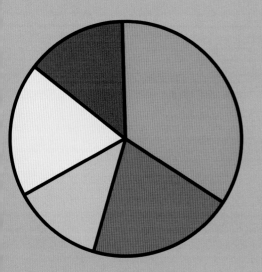

- QUICK
- PASSIONATE
- PHILOSOPHICAL
- ADVENTUROUS
- IMPATIENT

LIKES	DISLIKES
Yoga retreats	Feeling restless
Vape pens	Being told what to do
A good time	Debbie-downers

SKILLS	STRUGGLES
Taking risks	Anticipating challenges
Being the expert	Indecisiveness
Starting from scratch	Staying in place

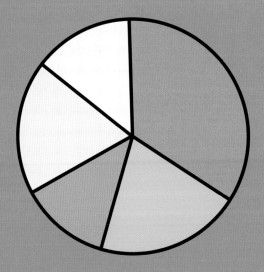

- EXPRESSIVE
- INSTINCTIVE
- PASSIONATE
- PERSUASIVE
- WITTY

CAREER

Sagittarius works to live, not the other way around. You know what life's about and you know it's not about working your fingers to the bone for superficial markers of success. However, if your career is connected to your passions in life, you'll pursue accomplishments to the ends of the earth. Your distaste for the routine doesn't connote laziness; it's actually the opposite! You get things done with all the energy of the fire sign you are. The world tells us we have to finish our homework before we go out and play, so you will work hard even if it's only because you can't wait to go sing karaoke at five o'clock. Low-key adrenaline junkies, Sagittarian office mates might procrastinate, but when push comes to shove, they often pull out a last-minute miracle. Your honest, straightforward nature robs you of the ability to feign interest in things that bore you. Seek out the adventure in every project to spark your tenacious intellect.

Adventure is where your head is at, Sagittarius, and that free spirit is contagious to those around you. You naturally disarm boundaries through laughter and allow people to be themselves. When it comes down to it, you are a fierce and loyal friend, who will protect the people that you love and care about. Depending on where Sagittarius is located in your chart, your energy, quick wit, and good nature will manifest themselves differently. Your dynamic character makes it easy for you to fit into different situations both socially and professionally.

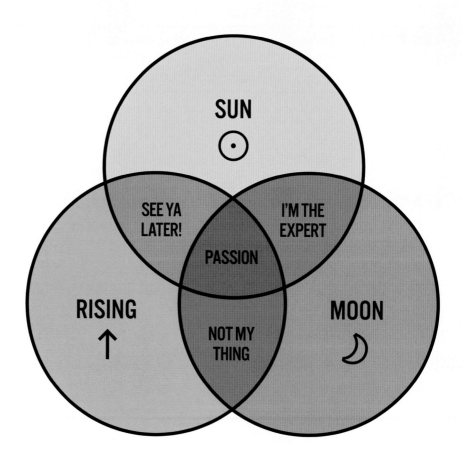

The sun is the core of your personality, and it illuminates the parts of your life that are most important to you. The placement of the moon in your chart influences your innermost self, the parts of you that condition the way you feel about yourself and the world. Your rising sign is the picture you paint of yourself when meeting new people and when you're in new situations. It's like the astrology version of a profile picture.

SAGITTARIUS SUN

If your sun shines in Sagittarius, the foundation of your personality is an energetic, optimistic seeker. You are inspired by new experiences in new places. With a bit of a restless nature, you can get bored easily and it can be difficult to hold your attention. Like the archer that represents your sign, your arrow is always pointing toward a target in the distance, and your focus follows your eye. You have an inherently bright sense of humor and you're quick to crack a joke. You're open-minded, but you can sometimes make snap judgments. The people around you value your honest nature and your joyful spirit.

SAGITTARIUS MOON

Lunar Sagittarians' deepest selves are defined by a basic need for freedom and plenty of space to grow. One of the happiest and most chill placements for the moon, Sagittarius moons are easy to love. They wake up excited to meet the day. They always need to be moving and hate to be pinned down. Trying to box in a lunar Sag is the quickest way to drive them away. Classic fire-sign competitiveness is present. Sag moons can get carried away with their drive to conquer new lands and come out on top of any competition. However, a Sag moon hates conflict and tends to run from a confrontation. A mutable sign, they are easily adaptable, and indulging their spontaneous streak makes them feel alive.

ADVENTUROUS   NON-COMMITTAL
HUMOROUS   OBLIVIOUS

SAGITTARIUS RISING

If you're a Sag rising, your image is that of a hopeful, enthusiastic adventure-seeker who loves to learn new things. You vibrate at a high frequency and can come off as having a lot of nervous energy. And yes, you might be nervous, but you're also just like an arrow in an archer's bow hand, full of momentum just waiting to be released. You love to have a task to occupy yourself with in every situation. Honest (sometimes to a fault), you tell people how you're feeling and what you think. Some might call you naive, but you choose to see the best in others and, generally, in yourself. You love a big promise, a sudden fiasco, a grandly harebrained goose chase. Like the archer that represents your sign, everyone that meets you notices that far-off glint in your eye, like you see something just over the horizon that is calling your name.

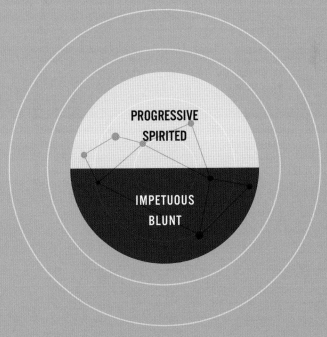

PROGRESSIVE
SPIRITED

IMPETUOUS
BLUNT

EARLY BIRD	NIGHT OWL	BE UR OWN IDOL	NO IS A SENTENCE	TIME IS MONEY
I'M AWARE	MADE MY OWN LUCK	BARK 'N BITE	I INSPIRE MYSELF	BITCOIN RESEARCH
I'LL DO IT	DAD JOKES	Free	HIGH MAINTENANCE	RESTING BOSS FACE
OLD SOUL	SIDE HUSTLE	EYE CONTACT	RISE & GRIND	LEFT BRAIN
I'LL TAKE IT	"PER MY LAST EMAIL"	BRAINSTORM	ELEVATOR PITCH	"SLACK ME"

Capricorn

DATES	ELEMENT	MODALITY
December 22–January 19	Earth	Cardinal

Just like the goat that your sign is represented by, you live in the world with all four hooves on the ground. Oh, right, we mean feet. And we know you only have two. And sometimes you have a fish tail for swimming through the nonsense. You get the gist, sensible sea-goat. You have a stable approach to life and you're focused on achieving your goals. You spend your energy on things you deem worthwhile and you find frivolity wasteful and boring. Like your fellow earth signs, Taurus and Virgo, you care more about the demands of the real, material world than you do about the loftier things in life.

Sag's explorative and spontaneous energy that seeks knowledge for knowledge's sake is taken down to earth when Capricorn season comes along. Cap energy loves knowledge and loves to conquer new challenges, but not for the joy of the journey. Of all earth signs, you are the one most drawn to the luxuries

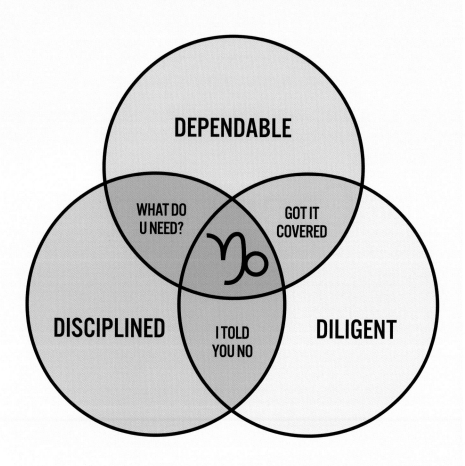

that the material world offers. For you, a goal isn't reached until the world cele-
brates your accomplishment. Sure, you want to achieve great things, but it's just
as important for you to be recognized for your achievements.

Let's be specific about recognition. We're talking M-O-N-E-Y, trophies,
and accolades—all the symbols of status that society has to offer. Don't be shy,
Capricorn; this doesn't mean you're shallow or materialistic (although that is a

risk for an unbalanced Cap). It is more a reflection of your need to feel useful in the world and to receive due recognition for your contributions. You value an equal exchange of effort and reward above all. You don't want to be rewarded for nothing. It's in your nature to work hard, but that hard work feels like it's all for nothing unless you are sure that others value your contributions.

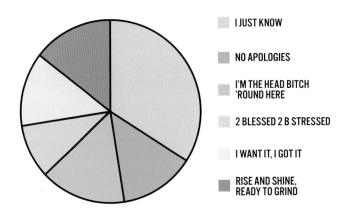

- I JUST KNOW
- NO APOLOGIES
- I'M THE HEAD BITCH 'ROUND HERE
- 2 BLESSED 2 B STRESSED
- I WANT IT, I GOT IT
- RISE AND SHINE, READY TO GRIND

You have an excellent poker face, but as a Capricorn you might find gambling a waste of resources. Speaking of resources, you're the most resourceful sign in the zodiac, bar none. You use whatever you have access to and somehow you make it work. You are dependable, and you always show up prepared for any situation. Moving day? You remember to buy the bubble wrap and save the day. Best friend going through a breakup? You show up with puzzles and junk food and tons of jokes about her ex's taste in music (it sucked). Speaking of jokes, you've got a lot of them. Your dry sense of humor is another lovable Capricorn trait. A few more for the road? Go-getter spirit. Single-minded focus on goals and values. And overall, just very cool.

RELATIONSHIPS

Although Capricorn is arguably the hardest working sign in the zodiac, you tend to take a cooler approach to love and relationships. Caps would prefer potential lovers to see them at their best, making money, achieving goals, and appearing to have it all put together. You want to be admired for the things that you pride yourself on. You are just as practical in matters of the heart as you are in the rest of your life. You're not one to enter into a messy fling on the down-low with a friend's ex. You feel most secure with realistic timelines and outcomes, and planning is one of your love languages. Although you're rarely lovestruck in a visible way, you have a deeply romantic soul and desire intimate bonds that you can rely on for a lifetime. Loving a Capricorn means being down to be patient and responsible. But once Cap falls in love, you can count on a secure and stable partnership that will never be clouded with doubt about where things are headed.

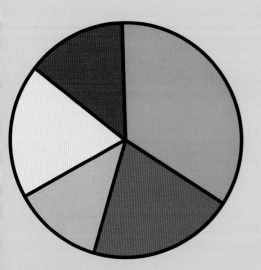

- DILIGENT
- DEPENDABLE
- AMBITIOUS
- CONTROLLING
- CONFIDENT

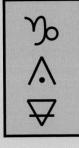

LIKES	DISLIKES
When things go as planned	The incompetence of others
Saving money	Missing out on a deal
Being in charge	Ignored advice

SKILLS	STRUGGLES
Making a plan	Collaborating with others
Building resources	Accepting praise
Long-term strategy	Diplomacy

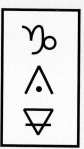

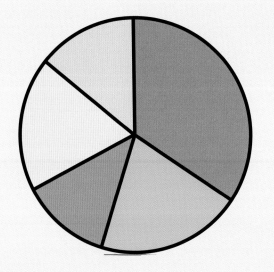

- PREPARED
- RESPONSIBLE
- PROTECTIVE
- PRACTICAL
- DRIVEN

CAREER

In the working world, Capricorn thrives when they can show off their aptitude for organization, consistent effort, and total focus on the goal they've set. "Showing off" is the operative word here. Caps need to be recognized, affirmed, and rewarded for their efforts. To keep a Capricorn motivated, there needs to be a clear upward trajectory in their career path. Cap is unsettled by nebulous, uncertain opportunities. Cap prefers a more traditional path to success with clearly outlined steps. To Capricorn, reinventing the wheel is one of the worst ways to spend their energy. It's inefficient, and no one will clap for you. The key to choosing the right career for Capricorn is to choose a role where their demand for excellence (from themselves and everyone around them) is rewarded with financial security, public acclaim, and a clear path to the top.

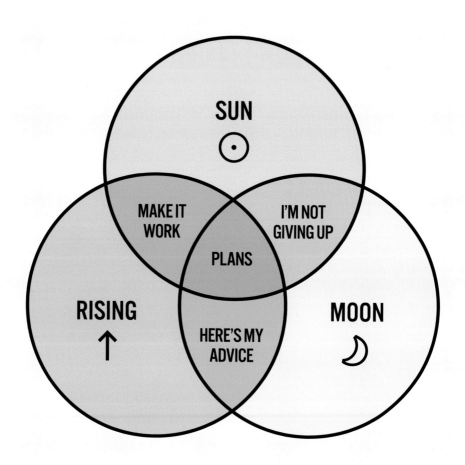

Always an overachiever, we know you're not done with your astrological learning yet! Depending on where Capricorn turns up in your chart, all that go-getter Cap energy manifests a bit differently. The sun in your chart is the gravitational center of your personality, the placement of the moon indicates your emotional needs, and your rising sign is the surface you show the world. Don't worry, there won't be an exam at the end.

CAPRICORN SUN

All the other planets and aspects orient around the sun. With the sun in Capricorn, your center is extremely sturdy and focused. You play your cards close to your chest and move through the world with sure-footed steps. You have a high level of integrity when it comes to your core values—hard work, usefulness, and singularity of purpose. Your highest satisfaction in life is derived from consistent effort toward a goal that you believe is truly worthwhile. You have a strongly future-oriented disposition and plan for all possible outcomes. You will rarely fail to achieve a goal because you won't quit until you do. All you want in return is worldly recognition and maybe an occasional parade or gala held in your honor. Is that so much to ask?!

DILIGENT STUBBORN
CARETAKING CONTROLLING

CAPRICORN MOON

If you're a Capricorn moon, contentment comes from maintaining a sense that you are productive and valuable. Others perceive your emotional world as neatly and competently under control. In your relationships, both personal and professional, you come off as a reliable, steady presence. However, you may feel lonely even when you're surrounded by others. The loneliness of this placement comes from the resistance to sharing who you actually are, warts and all. If you don't let people see you fully, you'll never feel like anyone knows you—because you haven't given them a chance! Lunar Capricorn's tendency to keep a cool head in all situations can lead to misunderstandings. Just because a lunar Capricorn has rationalized all their feelings and can present them in a measured, reasonable way does not necessarily mean that all is well in their hearts. Capricorn moons often need to work on vulnerability and learning not just how to explain their feelings but how to feel their feelings, especially in the company of trusted others. At the same time, you Cap moons out there should give yourselves big pats on the back for your consistent effort to remain calm, cool, and collected in the face of any challenge.

AMBITIOUS
HARD WORKING

COLD
DISTANT

CAPRICORN RISING

This sign also points to your mannerisms and style, all of the outward expressions of who you are. For Capricorn rising people, the vibe that comes across most is that of someone who has this whole "life" thing pretty well figured out. You have always been the responsible one in any group of friends. You have a clear respect for family and tradition. A Cap rising is the cousin that shows up to the holidays with an armful of cookies from a recipe that your great-grandmother used to make. Cap rising is not big on *bragging*, per se, but they are not shy when it comes to discussing their success—never in a tacky way! More like, informing you of their accomplishments in a nonchalant, tasteful way. Cap rising tends to be serious but very funny in a deadpan way. It's their sense of timing and their ability to keep a straight face all the way to the punchline. (PS: You don't want to play against a Cap rising in a poker match.)

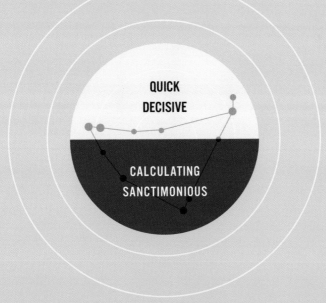

#NOTANALIEN	ALOOF AF	DISCOVERIES!	LOST IN WIKIPEDIA	FUTURE VISION
INNOVATION	WEIRD. I LIKE IT.	BUY WHY?	#ABSTRACT	PUNK 4 LYFE
HUMANITARIAN	LET'S GO TO SPACE	Free	RULES R 4 BREAKING	#PROGRESS
BEEN THERE, DONE THAT	ELECTRICITY!	GALAXY BRAIN	MY KICKSTARTER	BIGGER PICTURE
ECLECTIC TASTES	AUTHENTIC	AGAIN, WHY?	FOR SCIENCE!	PLATINUM PLS

Aquarius

DATES	ELEMENT	MODALITY
January 20–February 18	Air	Fixed

You'd think with a name like "Aquarius" you would be an emotion-centered water sign, but nope! Always full of surprises, Aquarius is the last air sign in the zodiac, represented by the water-bearer, the healer who pours this life-giving resource onto the land with the desire that all creatures should thrive. Fundamentally oriented toward all things revolutionary and avant-garde, you are always a few steps ahead of everyone else.

You have an even more rebellious heart than your fellow free-thinking air signs. It's very like an Aquarius to have a problem with authority and be bored to tears by conventional ways of doing things. People are always surprised by your latest eccentric hobby or your sudden sporadic veganism. It's no wonder that Uranus, the celestial ruler of innovation, technology, and surprises, also rules Aquarius.

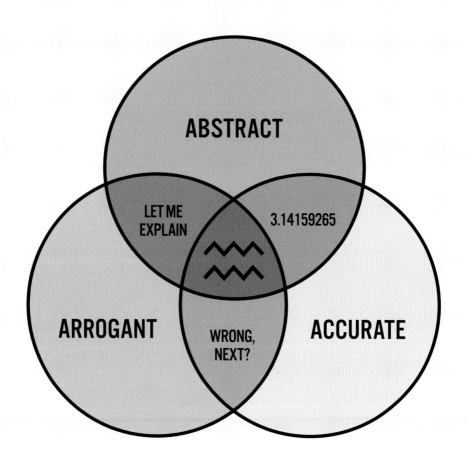

Aquarius takes Capricorn's drive to get exactly what they want in life and applies those high ideals to all of humanity. Where Capricorn will work their fingers to the bone to achieve their dreams, you will spend all your energy trying to make a fairer world where everyone's dreams are achievable without burning themselves out, yourself included.

If you haven't guessed by now, Aquarius is all about earth-shattering big ideas. With all of your energy being poured into the good of humankind, you struggle to find the purpose behind some of the everyday maintenance required to be a person. Things like washing your dishes right after you're done, texting your friends back, and remembering your partner's birthday can all fall by the wayside (especially if these tasks are framed as a chore or an obligation).

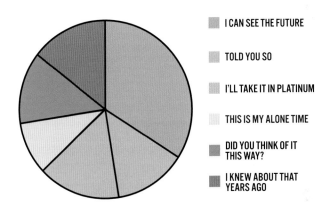

- I CAN SEE THE FUTURE
- TOLD YOU SO
- I'LL TAKE IT IN PLATINUM
- THIS IS MY ALONE TIME
- DID YOU THINK OF IT THIS WAY?
- I KNEW ABOUT THAT YEARS AGO

Aquarius thrives when they feel totally free to express themselves. You love to be part of a team where everyone is equally invested in each other's well-being. You are at your best when surrounded by passionate, like-minded people. You trust like-minded people with a strong sense of justice who don't attempt to make you into something you're not. And if anyone wants to try and rein in your eccentric ways, they're gonna need a lot of luck.

RELATIONSHIPS

There is no playbook for an Aquarius in love. Each relationship dynamic is made up as it goes along. You see, Aquarius is not the biggest fan of rules. That doesn't necessarily make Aquarius an unreliable partner. An Aquarius is likely to have their own particular ways of doing things that line up with their convictions about the world. Even though they don't put much stock in the rules of society, they have a strong moral compass, and integrity ranks high on their list of foundational values. Aquarius is deeply invested in their partner's well-being on every level. If Aquarius is prominent in your chart, you'll find you have passion in abundance. You need a partner that you connect with intellectually. This doesn't just mean finding someone who also wants to talk about carbon emissions and watch *Jeopardy!* reruns with you (although, that would definitely be a plus!). You need to feel that you can form a genuine friendship with a potential love interest. Aquarian energy is all about finding a shared passion for making the world a better place and your shared time together as uniquely enjoyable as possible.

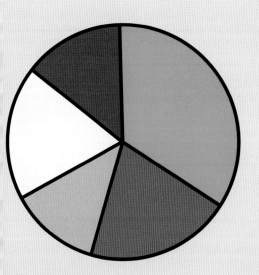

- **AUTHENTIC**
- **RESERVED**
- **INTELLIGENT**
- **HUMANITARIAN**
- **CONTRADICTORY**

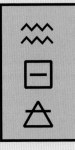

LIKES	DISLIKES
Inventing things	Same shit, different day
Helping you understand	Tradition
Being fascinated	Limitation

SKILLS	STRUGGLES
Predicting the outcome	Working with details
Understanding complexity	Accepting criticism
Awareness of multiple perspectives	Consistency

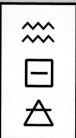

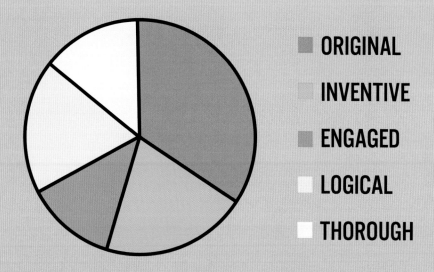

- ORIGINAL
- INVENTIVE
- ENGAGED
- LOGICAL
- THOROUGH

CAREER

One of the greatest Aquarian skill sets at work is their ability to handle anything that's thrown at them with their signature chill demeanor. Aquarius is a master of the here and now, able to zoom in on the work in front of them without feeling overwhelmed. Aquarius follows their gut and has a strong internal sense of direction. They march to the beat of their own drum, and sometimes that drum is beating out a high-flying dance beat when the rest of the team is plodding along to a marching band. That said, Aquarius resents red tape and hates to play by the rules. Learning to navigate the unavoidable bureaucracies of the working world will be challenging for Aquarius. Their individualistic nature can be their greatest asset under the right conditions. If you give an Aquarius the freedom to find their own way through a project, they will rarely disappoint.

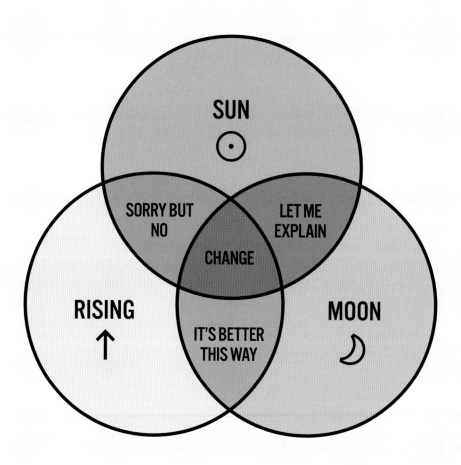

As a lover of new ideas, Aquarius, we want to give you a little more food for thought. To find out more about the way Aquarian energy manifests in your personality, learn about the subtle differences between Aquarius sun, moon, and rising.

AQUARIUS SUN

The placement of the sun in your chart is all about your life's journey to becoming your most authentic self. If the sun is in Aquarius in your chart, this journey is all about discovering the meaning of freedom in your life. You are the most inventive sign in the zodiac and you possess a uniquely innovative perspective. You bring people together and once they've arrived, you hold their attention with surprising and titillating ideas. Pushing boundaries, dismantling oppressive systems, and finding a better way for humanity to live are all on the Aquarius to-do list. The key for you, Aquarius? You must begin with yourself. Liberate your mind from thought patterns and beliefs that limit you or make you feel small. This is the necessary self-reflection that will help you lead others to their freedom and ultimately make your dreams a reality.

PROGRESSIVE UNPREDICTABLE
INVENTIVE PROUD

AQUARIUS MOON

The placement of the moon in your chart points to your emotional nature and the ways that you feel fulfilled and comfortable in your life. When the moon wanders into Aquarius territory, you have a rebel on your hands. The soul of a lunar Aquarius is all about ripping off band-aids and poking at tender emotions. Aquarius is oriented toward living in a better future, which means that they are often frustrated with the status quo. They tend to be emotionally tumultuous because they care so deeply about growth and transformation. To soothe the stormy seas of a lunar Aquarian's heart, they need ample space to channel their energy into their idiosyncratic hobbies and passions. This frees up some of their heart space so that they can give and receive love on a personal level, rather than just from their characteristic big-picture perspective.

UNIQUE · DETACHED

FRIENDLY · AWKWARD

AQUARIUS RISING

Your rising sign is often described as the mask you wear in public. If your rising sign is Aquarius, that mask would be *quite* the conversation starter. True rebels are utterly entertaining if you're on their level; it's safe to say that you definitely want an Aquarius rising at your next party. These freethinkers are often hilarious because of their ability to make quick and surprising connections that others would miss. Offbeat and passionate about humanitarian pursuits, they are likely to talk your ear off about their latest hobby that you've never even heard of. Although their fresh perspective can be jarring to more conventional types, you'll always want an Aquarius rising on speed dial for those times when all the normal solutions to a problem haven't yielded results and you're ready for your mind to be blown.

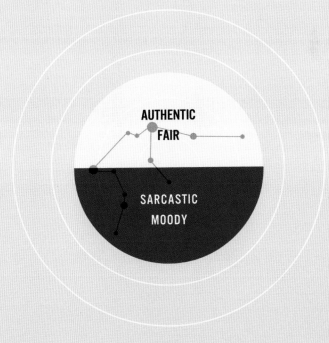

AUTHENTIC

FAIR

SARCASTIC

MOODY

BOUNDARIES?	SAD PLAYLIST	#FEELS	CONFUSED PLAYLIST	DREAM JOURNAL
HOLD ME?	MADE U A POTION	ART THERAPY	WHO AM I?	HEALING
HOW DO YOU FEEL?	LUCID DREAMS	Free	DRINK WATER!!	COLORS!
CREATIVE AF	NAP TIME	BATH TIME	WINE ANYONE?	YOU CAN TELL ME
EMPATHETIC AF	KLEENEX	MY CRYSTALS	CONNECTION	HAPPY PLAYLIST

Pisces

DATES	ELEMENT	MODALITY
February 19–March 20	Water	Mutable

Pisces takes to astrology like a fish in water. (Sorry! The pun was just so easy!) It's true, as the most psychic sign of the zodiac, you are already inclined toward soul-searching and self-knowledge that astrology offers us. Intuitive, emotionally intelligent, and given to daydreams and strong moods, Pisces is the mutable water sign that wears its heart on its sleeve. As the last constellation in the zodiac, Pisces has learned from all the signs that came before, and with that knowledge comes a deep sensitivity and compassion for all other living beings. Represented by two fish swimming in opposite directions, you live with one foot in reality and one foot firmly planted in the watery depths of fantasy and feeling.

With Neptune—the planet that governs creativity and dreams—as your sign's ruler, you have an expansive imagination and are more than likely a gifted creative type. However, Neptune is a tricky master. If allowed to run wild, Neptune's

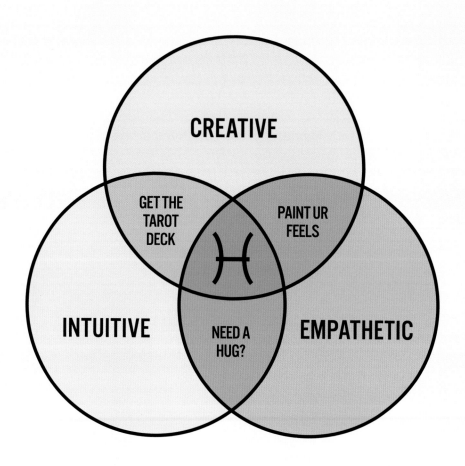

influence can lead to illusions, deception, and escapism. It's important to find people or practices that ground you in reality. You need to push yourself to stay present in the here and now.

With all the lessons learned by the other signs floating around in your head and heart, you have the gift (or, sometimes, the burden) of communicating your insights to the world around you. This can be challenging for you, Pisces, because you are so empathetic that you can get overwhelmed by other people's feelings. You're an emotional and psychic sponge, and you can't share your gifts with the world unless you have a clear sense of where you start and where others begin. To stay healthy, you've got to balance your ethereal inner world with the demands of the material world.

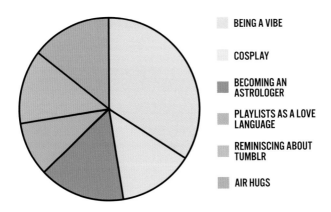

BEING A VIBE

COSPLAY

BECOMING AN ASTROLOGER

PLAYLISTS AS A LOVE LANGUAGE

REMINISCING ABOUT TUMBLR

AIR HUGS

Like your fellow water signs (Scorpio and Cancer), you are definitely in touch with your emotions. As the mutable sibling of the water trio, you tend to adjust more easily to your surroundings and come off as less intense than the others. Where Scorpio and Cancer may seem a little standoffish, you overflow. You are generous and you have an optimistic view of humanity, even with all the psychic weight you carry. You're excited by spiritual exploration, and you help the people around you to turn inward and reflect. A lover of romance, art, music, and expression, people are drawn to your creative nature.

RELATIONSHIPS

When you have the love of a Pisces, you will know it. The most sensitive sign in the sky, Pisces has *a lot* of space and time to daydream about you and all the ways to make you happy. This ethereal empath is all about heart-to-heart conversations, love poems, candle-lit dinners. Pisces is also pretty conflict-averse and prefers to escape to their own imagination rather than address issues head-on.

If you've seen an over-the-top date in a rom-com, Pisces has probably done it or considered doing it. If you find yourself falling for a Pisces, take note: they crave this same level of romantic engagement. In relationships, a Pisces will always support you in making your hopes and dreams a reality. They can empathize with your passion and completely get behind it as if it were their own. That's just who Pisces is.

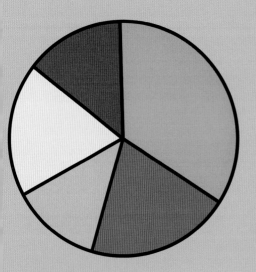

- FORGIVING
- INTUITIVE
- ADAPTABLE
- FORGETFUL
- INDULGENT

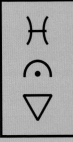

LIKES	DISLIKES
Transcending the mortal coil	Matters of fact
Free hugs	Rigid people
A well-timed rainbow	"Sugar free"

SKILLS	STRUGGLES
Out of the box thinking	Separating head and heart
Emotional intelligence	Taking it personally
Responsive to feedback	Staying focused

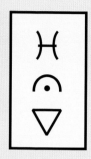

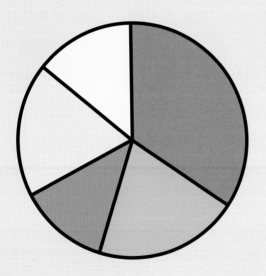

- INTROSPECTIVE
- MULTI-TALENTED
- CREATIVE
- RECEPTIVE
- PASSIONATE

CAREER

If your workplace were an orchestra, with many different people all playing their own notes but together forming a single song, then Pisces would be a soloist with a strong improvisational streak. Pisces are guided by their intuition and can resent being told what to do and when to do it. Unlike their air sign cousin Aquarius (the zodiac's ultimate rebel), Pisces resists the chain of command because it's so foreign to Pisces's self-guided and intuitive nature that it just seems ridiculous.

As the mutable water sign, Pisces is highly adaptable and may change careers a few times in their life, but they are so in touch with their intuitive gifts that the choices they make will often lead them to a place that is more in line with their soul's path than it is with mainstream values. Pisces loves to get lost in a project and feel their way through it. They crave recognition and need to feel as if they are being listened to and appreciated. Although Pisces is not one for corporate culture or professional optics, if Pisces truly believes in what they're doing, they have a deep well of energy and work ethic to devote to their career.

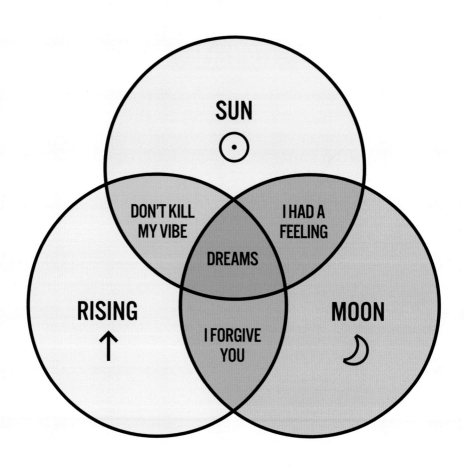

Wasn't that a wild ride, Pisces? We know you don't shy away from an opportunity to dig deeper, so here are a few insights to ponder. If your sun, moon, or rising sign is Pisces, your dreamy energy could manifest in a few different ways.

PISCES SUN

When the sun swims into Pisces in a person's chart, it signals a deep need for spiritual completion. As the final sign of the zodiac, Pisces is entranced by their own path toward spiritual awakening. If your sun is in Pisces, it can be challenging to move through the material world, tending to the normal human stuff like bills and meal prep and . . . hey! Pisces, are you listening? Or did you get lost in a daydream the minute you read "bills"? The sun in your chart indicates your basic tendencies and the places where growth is necessary and possible. For you, this is all about balancing your spiritual insights with the demands of the present moment. At your best, you have the most empathetic and generous heart, almost overflowing with compassion. Make sure to pour that into your cup first, so that you can keep showing up the way you want to.

FORGIVING DELUSIONAL
ADAPTABLE ESCAPIST

PISCES MOON

The moon rules your dreamy side, the part of you that feels, imagines, and inspires. If the moon in your chart is in Pisces, you have a rich fantasy world that you escape to when you are overwhelmed. You fall in love easily and you feel intensely. Your emotional world is complex and encompasses all the signs of the zodiac that came before you. It's no wonder you can seem lost in thought more often than not! While other people just experience their own perspective and their own feelings, you dwell in the prismatic experience of everyone's emotions all at once. To stay sane, it is important to create healthy boundaries and to find ways to ground yourself. Learn to love a little alone time—journal, paint, just take a bath and listen to music. Whatever it takes to share your insights with the world.

PISCES RISING

Your rising sign guides the impression you make on people. If you're a Pisces rising, you have the unique ability to adapt to your surroundings. Chalk that up to Pisces's mutable water-sign vibes and all that empathy. Pisces can walk into a room and immediately sense what everyone needs and then deliver it to them on a silver platter. If you need a shoulder to cry on, Pisces rising is your best friend. If you need to laugh off a hard week and unwind, Pisces is your best friend. Pisces rising is a social chameleon that can transform into exactly what is called for in any situation. This gift for drawing others to you and putting them at ease is irresistible. But make sure not to fall too deeply under your own spell. When you go home at the end of the night, make sure you remember who you were when you left the house.

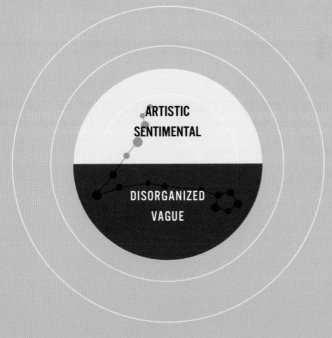

ARTISTIC
SENTIMENTAL

DISORGANIZED
VAGUE

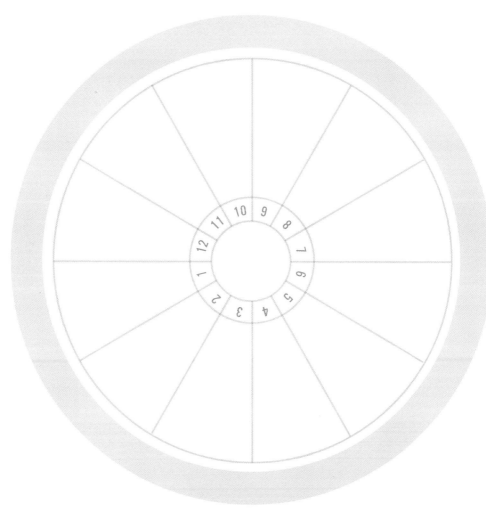

Fill in this blank birth chart to match what you find in the app for easy reference!

THE STARS ARE YOURS NOW.

You may not be an astrologer yet, but this book has taken you on a journey through the universe of you. You and your birth chart are full of infinite possibilities and paths to explore. If you want to go deeper, there's a whole world of astrology waiting for you to dive into. You'll find more resources in the Sanctuary app, and there are many brilliant astrologers to learn from through their birth chart readings and teachings.

Don't stop here—your chart has plenty to keep you busy for a lifetime. The stars and planets are always on the move. Each day, each moment presents new circumstances that activate your unique birth chart in special ways. People have used this combination of birth chart and daily astrological circumstances for millennia—to find love, to select important days for new journeys, to heal, and to commune with the universe at large. You don't need to be an astrologer to get guidance from the movements of the sky, but the insights of an expert can always help. Don't be shy about looking for an astrologer who can help you understand your chart or your journey. Try a birth chart reading and see what clarity that conversation can bring you.

Astrology is an opportunity for connection and context for your path through life. Whether you connect most with the moon cycle or are looking to confront the latest retrograde, think of the astrological cycles as a celestial weather report we all share. Tracking them helps you understand what's going on outside yourself. Your birth chart in turn is a guide to how those movements might impact you. As the world keeps turning, you keep growing and changing under the watchful gaze of the stars. It's positively cosmic, and that's how we like it.

Index

ACKNOWLEDGMENTS

The Sanctuary team would like to thank our wonderful agents Richard Pine and Eliza Rothstein at Inkwell Management.

We also thank the team at Sacks & Co., especially Carla Sacks, Reid Kutrow, Samantha Tillman and Kate Rakvic.

We are deeply appreciative of the team at Sanctuary, including Ross and Adam, whose ongoing support helped clear the way for this book, and Emily, Kristina, and Jeanna, who laid the groundwork for what Sanctuary, and this book, could be. Without all of you, this book would not have been possible.

Individually, we'd also like to thank . . .

To the astrologers who lent me their expertise and time, thank you. Thanks as well to my writing group, who keep me sane. And grateful forever to E, who helps me see the stars. —HEDH

I am grateful to my mother and my brothers first and forever. To E & N who are always the reason. And to my partner T, who is a very good boy. —SPB

I'd like to thank the members of the astrological community that I've had the pleasure of working with. And thank you to my roommate, my cat, my boyfriend, and all the video games that keep me sane. —SB

Thank you to Matt for your calming presence, and to my sun in Pisces for always guiding me toward creative endeavors. —CB

Sanctuary Team:
Ross Clark, CEO
Haley ED Houseman, Director of Content & Brand
Adam Lampell, Vice President, Operations & Business Development
Cassandra Chernin, Head of Growth
Daniel Scally, Head of Engineering
Sterling Bowen, Social Media Manager
Claire Berner, Graphic Designer

Development Team:
Sarah Panliburtion Barnes, Developmental Editor
Haley E.D. Houseman, Developmental Editor
Sterling Bowen, Developmental Contributor
Claire Berner, Developmental Designer

ABOUT THE AUTHOR

Sanctuary is on a mission to bring the mystical into the digital age with an app designed to help you explore your cosmic curiosity. Find their daily horoscopes and mystical experts wherever you are, all with a tap on your phone. There are new features to discover all the time, so dive in and start your journey!

Making traditional astrology accessible is just one way they bring the modern to the mystical. They're reinventing the traditional birth chart reading with interactive birth charts and on-demand chatting with astrologers who can help you read your chart.

For more timely astrology content, find the app on social media with more than 1.3 million followers on Instagram, where you can catch signature astrology information every day. You can also find them daily on Spotify's "Horoscope Today" podcast.

The app has been featured in *New York Magazine's The Cut, The New York Times,* the *Los Angeles Times, Bloomberg, Wired, Refinery29, SELF* and *Vogue,* among other publications, and has been recognized for its expertise by audiences around the world. For more information, check out www.sanctuaryworld.co and follow us on social @sanctuarywrld.

Scan to download the app.